Carter G. Woodson's
Appeal

Carter G. Woodson, 1915.

Carter G. Woodson's Appeal

by
Carter G. Woodson

Edited with an Introduction by

Daryl Michael Scott

The ASALH Press
Washington, DC

The ASALH Press
Washington, DC

Editor's Dedication

To my late mother, Mary E. Scott. *Along with every-thing else, thanks for instilling in me that old-school racial pride that Woodson's disciples passed on to you at Douglas Elementary and Wendell Phillips High.*

To the memory of my late grandmother, Velma Brown. Born in Alabama a half century after the destruction of slavery and only a few months before Woodson established the Association, my grandmother grew up almost wholly without the benefit of schools. Granny proved to be too much for anybody--black or white, male or female, Northerner or Southerner --who set out to hold her down and bend her will to theirs. She passed away, December 14, 2007. *God keeps us now, Granny Grip.*

Contents

Acknowledgements

The assistance of Atty. Laura Wilkinson of Weil, Gotshal, and Manges has been invaluable. I was working on copyright information about *The Mis-Education of the Negro* with her when I discovered the manuscript. Had she not given so freely of her time, "The Case of the Negro" would still be lost.

Gloria Harper Dickinson gave me the opportunity to keep a personal pledge to help "save ASALH," and she has taught me some things about spirituality. *Yes, Gloria, finding this manuscript has been a blessing.*

Marilyn Thomas-Houston aided me on technical aspects of this project--as she has on many others. *Your father would be amazed at the number of trades and professions you've mastered.*

I want to give a special thanks to Ka'mal McClarin and Daniel Broyold, my research assistants at Howard University. Ka'mal has lived Woodson with me for several years. Barbara Dunn read and commented on a draft of the manuscript, providing corrections and inspiration. Tahlia Day's editing services proved invaluable, visit www.katharosediting.com. Abdur-Rahman Muhammad took time from his own important manuscript to lend a hand. My other assistant, Joy Savannah Scott, deserves a special mention for her typing, editorial advice, and patience with a distracted father. *Thanks, Joy-Joy. And you are not the first child of ASALH who will go on to do important things. Remember, our institutions matter.*

Daryl Michael Scott
Upper Marlboro, Maryland
December 21, 2007

Editor's Preface

I discovered Carter G. Woodson's unpublished manuscript on a Saturday afternoon during the summer of 2005 among the records of the Association for the Study of African American Life and History (AS-ALH), formerly the Association for the Study of Negro Life and History (ASNLH). It was in a storage bay filled with file cabinets and boxes, which contained a part of ASALH's nine decades of records. At the time, I was working on a project to protect ASALH's intellectual property. In 1969, Charles Wesley, one of the great African American institutionalists of the twentieth century, had edited a new version of Woodson's *The Mis-Education of the Negro*, silently adding material to secure a new copyright that others could republish only at their own peril. I was looking for the material that made up what a crew of Howard University graduate students and I had taken to calling "Wesley's web." My eleven-year-old daughter, Joy Savannah

Scott, was with me, reading and waiting patiently as her father whiled away her afternoon on yet another ASALH project.

I was searching through the files of Rayford Logan, the late Howard University professor and the Association's executive director after the death of Carter G. Woodson. I came upon an envelope. The writing was unmistakably Woodson's. Inside was a manuscript in typescript. It was entitled "The Case of the Negro." The title page made clear that Woodson had authored the text, and I instantly knew he had never published it. Here was a lost-now-found manuscript by the Father of Black History!

It took a little work, but I was able to convince Joy that her Saturday afternoon in a dirty, musty storage unit had not been a waste.

***

In editing Woodson's manuscript, I have chosen to produce a book that will be attractive to as wide an audience as possible. While I have added footnotes to illuminate obscure references and esoteric terminology, I have sought to produce a clean, readable text that will allow most readers to follow Woodson's social criticism without the intrusions of strikeouts, extensive editing symbols, and editorial comments.

Documentary work is neither my inclination nor specialty, and such projects rarely receive the public attention they deserve. Moreover, Woodson remains of great interest to the general public still enamored of his *The Mis-Education of the Negro*. It has been my intent to produce a volume that highlights Woodson's no-holds-barred style unencumbered by an overbearing scholarly apparatus.

Because I anticipate that some documentary scholar will eventually produce such an edition, I have edited the manuscript in the manner that enhances Woodson's perspective and arguments. The work was an advanced draft rather than a final manuscript. Redundant material has been removed, the language clarified, and the grammar corrected. Where Woodson's own comments in the margins questioned whether certain passages should be included, rewritten, expanded, or modified, I have made those editorial decisions. It is rather clear that Woodson had not intended to include footnotes. I have included them because I believe that not even many of Woodson's contemporaries would have known the authorities he alluded to in the text. I have also opted to change the title. I consider "The Case of the Negro," Woodson's working title, to be the untouched, unfinished manuscript. Only a photocopied presentation of the manuscript—replete with margin notes, strikeouts, and confusion about prospective changes—could carry that name. In general, I have proceeded as is often done when a manuscript is published posthumously. I have relied on my experience as a historian who has become quite familiar with his subject's corpus of writings.

In every sense but one, I have sought to be true to what I believe was Woodson's original intent. Woodson did not desire to publish this book. "The Case of the Negro," according to Woodson, had its origins in a request from two blacks prominent in the Young Men's Christian Association movement for African Americans. Channing Tobias and Jesse Moorland, the latter a member of the ASNLH's board, solicited Woodson to write a book to counter one written by W. D. Weatherford.[1] A powerful force in the YMCA movement and a well-known supporter of blacks, Weatherford was nonetheless a proponent of white superiority. His 1912 work, *Present Forces in Negro Progress*, constituted a sugary elixir of liberalism and racism written to address the race problem in America. Among other things, Weatherford wrote of blacks as a "tropical" race best fit for thriving in Africa.[2] Woodson stated that even though he was not much interested in being drawn into "the discussion of the race problem," he agreed to publish a book with the Association Press, the publishing house of the YMCA. When he finished his task, however, Moorland and Tobias backed out because "I was rather hard on preachers of a certain type," according to Woodson.

Although Moorland and Tobias changed their minds, Woodson could have published the book had he wanted. He was the majority stockholder in and the operational head of The Associated Publishers, a firm he incorporated in 1921, the year that he wrote this manuscript. Once established, his firm published all of his subsequent books. The commercial viability of the project would not have prevented Woodson from publishing it. When assessing a book for publication, he often elected to publish deserving titles even when he believed they would be commercial failures. In not publishing "The Case of the Negro," Woodson made a decision that obviously reflected his best judgment.

One can only speculate about why he decided against publishing it. Perhaps he simply desired to honor Moorland and Tobias's desire not to publish a work so critical of certain black ministers. Perhaps he realized the work had a polemical quality that would undermine his more scholarly efforts put forth through ASNLH and The Associated Publishers. This, of course, was his first inclination. At points in his appeal, he was more biting in his criticism than an effective advocate can afford to be. Certainly, the mirror that he held up to the faces of white Americans presented an unflattering image often born of their own shortcomings.

It is my sense that Woodson did not want to rile his funding sources at a crucial juncture in his labors. At the time, Woodson was the recipient of a grant from the Carnegie Foundation for $25,000 and had applied to the Laura Spelman Rockefeller Foundation for a similar amount, which he eventually secured. Adjusted for inflation, the total amounted to roughly $500,000. Two years earlier, he had left a deanship at Howard in a disagreement with the white president, J. Stanley Durkee, and was at odds with Thomas Jesse Jones, a white scholar who was a favorite of the foundations. The grants allowed him to resign from teaching and educational administration and devote his time fully to ASNLH.[3] Moreover, the salary was generous enough to allow him to live frugally and take the remainder to establish The Associated Publishers. Given his candid remarks about white culture and beliefs, this little volume would likely have drawn the ire of many powerful whites at the very worst moment.

Why he did not publish it later, I can hardly venture to say. Perhaps his shifting thought about the black elite, the changes in America and race relations, and his own intellectual interests made the book seem dated. As a work of social commentary, it is indeed a reflection of the 1920s, not the 1930s or 1940s. In any event, I have not found anything to shed light on Woodson's later thinking.

While the particular grounds for Woodson's decision are not known, I have decided that there are matters that favor the work's publication, regardless of Woodson's intent. It should be noted that Woodson did not destroy the manuscript in the nearly three decades that followed its creation. He kept it with his materials where it could be eventually found by his sometimes wayward protégé Rayford Logan or whoever followed in his footsteps at ASNLH. "The Case for the Negro" was among the property he left the Association. The fact that Logan never published the work probably stems from the fact that he resigned the directorship abruptly after roughly a year and a half.

The compelling reason for departing from Woodson's decision lies in the sheer historical importance of the man and the book. While Woodson was not vainglorious and never believed that his life would become of general interest to successive generations, Woodson, ever the historian, certainly recognized that what he left was indeed part of the historical record—published or unpublished. Woodson's intellectual and institutional contributions mark him as a major figure in twentieth-century American history. His *The Mis-Education of the Negro* ignited a firestorm that still smolders seventy-five years later. Few Americans have

created a cultural tradition as vibrant as Negro His-
tory Week, now Black History Month. Indeed, what
Woodson created captures the attention of 300 million
people for an entire month every year. While many
in the Association lament that Woodson is not better
known, millions of youth at least hear that he is the
Father of Black History and the Founder of Negro
History Week. The scholarly journal he founded, the
Journal of Negro History, now the *Journal of African
American History*, is the foundation of the field of
Black History and the discipline of Black Studies. It
is the oldest and most prestigious journal in the field.
Lastly, the organization that he created and stewarded
is the oldest scholarly society in the black world.

   Given this, Woodson's thoughts, as well as his ac-
tions, matter greatly and belong to those whose world
he shaped. In his social commentary, his force of personality rises forth from the page, speaking volumes
not only about the man and what motivated him but
also about the times in which he lived and labored.
The world needs to know what he thought about the
white folks for whom he intended this appeal. Written
at the onset of the New Negro cultural outpouring of
post-World War I America, *Woodson's Appeal* reflects
the spirit of the times—even if it might have been often
too caustic to let loose on its intended audience.

Notes

1 Carter G. Woodson, "A Rejoinder to Dr. Tobias," *The Chicago Defender,* July 30, 1932.

2 W. D. Weatherford, *Present Forces in Negro Progress* (New York: Association Press, 1912), 15.

3 Jacqueline Goggin, *Carter G. Woodson: A Life in Black History* (Baton Rouge: Louisiana State University Press, 1997).

Introduction

In African American intellectual history, there are two main currents of social criticism. The first is aimed at white society, faulting it for oppressing peoples of color, particularly African Americans. The second is internal criticism, critiques of the shortcomings within the group. Over the past two centuries, African Americans—one of the most literary peoples to ever inhabit the world—have produced countless essays of each kind.

For all the productivity, the classics of black social criticism are few. Among the critiques of white America, those which have stood the test of time are *David Walker's Appeal* and W. E. B. Du Bois's *Souls of Black Folk.*[1] Written during the early decades of the nineteenth century, *David Walker's Appeal*, as Walker's work has become known, outdistanced virtually all similar writings, and has become a central text among scholars in Black Studies and is quickly becoming a central text in American history. Walker, a free black operating out of Boston, caused a firestorm among slaveholders in the South, who feared that his antislavery broadside would incite the slaves to revolt. *Walker's Appeal* lives on because readers find in it an affirmation of black solidarity against slavery, a caustic critique of American hypocrisy on the question of liberty and equality, and an insight into the prophetic nature of African American Christian thought.

Writing almost a century later, W. E. B. Du Bois responded to the racial crisis of the later decades of the nineteenth century, which brought America to embrace the legalized segregation and disfranchisement of black Americans, to tolerate the lynching of African Americans, and to turn a blind eye to the economic exploitation of the second generation of freedpeople in the South. With lyrical prose, *The Souls of Black Folk* highlights the humanity of his oppressed people, including the failures of its dominant leadership group presided over by Booker T. Washington. Since its publication in 1903, intellectuals, black and white alike, have marveled at its literary quality and found Du Bois's plaintive prose alluring.

With its critique of Washington's leadership, Du Bois's *Souls* was something of a hybrid of internal and external criticism, but the racial self-criticism is mild indeed when compared with E. Franklin Frazier's

Black Bourgeoisie and Harold Cruse's *The Crisis of the Negro Intellectual.*[2] The ultimate integrationist text, Frazier's critique of the frivolity of the black middle class relied on ridicule to prod the black elite away from any tendency to self-segregation, which he called a "world of make believe." Only a decade later, Cruse's *Crisis* forced a generation of would-be revolutionaries to come to grips with their lack of theoretical sophistication.

Although known as the Father of Black History, Woodson is also well known for his contribution to African American self-criticism. A proponent of scientific history, Woodson produced scholarly works that were, as Du Bois once remarked, "'of the strict Harvard dryasdust school.'"[3] The facts, he believed, should and would speak for themselves. Few facts are inherently interesting, and Woodson's presentation had all the cold efficiency of the new age of science. In any event, few scholarly studies, including Du Bois's, remain of interest to subsequent generations of scholars, and neither Du Bois nor Woodson are well known to the reading public because of their scholarship. *The Souls of Black Folk* and *The Mis-Education of the Negro* are the books that have kept their names before readers.[4]

Few today realize that during the 1930s, Carter G. Woodson was one of the most prominent black public intellectuals. His essays and speeches were of great interest to African Americans. During the Great Depression, Du Bois lost control over *The Crisis,* the magazine that had made him well known. From the late 1920s forward, Woodson's articles could be found in Baltimore's *Afro-American,* Philadelphia's *Tribune, The St. Louis Argus, The New York Age,* and *The Boston Chronicle,* to name a few. He wrote about history, current events, and black leadership. Almost twenty years into his labors at the Association, Woodson hit his stride as a public figure.

The core of his message was that the middle-class was mis-educated, lacking knowledge of themselves as black people and thereby offering poor leadership to the black masses. Ironically, Woodson became exceedingly popular among the middle classes, who individually believed that Woodson was actually talking about somebody other than themselves. E. Franklin Frazier, of course, followed in Woodson's footsteps in making the black middle class the target of his criticism and the focus of most African American self-criticism. Unlike Du Bois, whose assumed readership for *Souls* was white, Woodson's imagined public was black, as one would expect of self-criticism. Whereas Du Bois's tone was plaintive and seeking acceptance from whites, Woodson's was the strongman tone that we associate with nationalism. Decidedly ethnic and racially proud, Woodson was not a nationalist. His goal was to realize racial equality and harmony within the American political context. Yet Woodson spoke to the ethnic and racial underpinnings of black nationalism, and this largely accounts for the enduring popularity of *The Mis-Education of the Negro,* an essay more than seventy-five years old.

Carter G. Woodson's Appeal is a markedly different work of social criticism against white oppression. In it one finds the stridently ethnic and racial pride that one hears in *David Walker's Appeal* rather than what George Frederickson once referred to as the "purple prose" of the *Souls of Black Folk*, the attempt to use sorrow to gain white sympathy. In a dispute with Du Bois, Woodson once said that he wrote like a child, undoubtedly referring to Du Bois's tendency of playing on the supposed tender sensibilities of his white readers.[5] In his criticism of white America, Woodson, in the tradition of David Walker, never overestimated the liberality of whites as a group. Further, Woodson, like Walker, never appeared to be hankering for individual acceptance.

Woodson's essay is hardly an appeal as most understand the term. Woodson gave his book the title, "The Case of the Negro," but it more often reads as "The Case against the White Man." In style and tone, it is as much a lawyerly indictment of white society as it is a defense of the black community. Addressing a white jury that has already reached its judgment based on prejudice, the race's advocate nowhere seeks to elicit their sympathy or pity, but throughout he points up the failings of the white community replete with sarcasm and open contempt. On behalf of his client, Woodson seeks only to set the record straight, to proclaim the black race falsely accused of a long list of groundless charges. At times Woodson makes clear that the charges against the black race would be more accurately imputed to the race sitting on the jury. Indeed, it reads almost as if Woodson's real audience is not the jury but the black public looking on from the Jim Crow gallery.

In 1921, when Woodson wrote his appeal, legal segregation and disfranchisement had been in place for more than a generation in most places in the South. In the famous words of one Southern writer, black people were "politically dead."[6] In the North and West, African Americans often exercised the right to vote, but whites exercised what was then their constitutional right to discriminate wantonly against blacks in all facets of life, especially in employment and housing. Going beyond their *rights*, Northern and Western whites also lynched blacks, chased them out of town, and subjected them to riots. Indeed, *Woodson's Appeal* was written in the aftermath of the wave of race riots that plagued America after World War I. Woodson's attitude, no doubt, was shaped by the fact that he witnessed and was almost a victim of the anti-black riot in the nation's capital in 1919.[7]

In the postwar era, Southern whites were determined to keep their political supremacy in place. The 1920s witnessed the rise of the second Ku Klux Klan movement. The new movement was largely urban rather than rural, and it was Northern as well as Southern. Modernization and rapid immigration had awakened white Protestant xenophobia, but it was combined with traditional anti-black racism.[8] The South continued to be a white man's country.

In the South, white liberalism was weak and feeble; it barely had a heartbeat. White "interracialists," as they were known, sought to curb the excesses of white supremacy by playing notions of Southern decency. For whites to remain the ruling race, it was not necessary, this small group of liberals argued, for African Americans to be wantonly lynched, for their children to be unschooled, and for their public institutions to be bereft of public funding. Hardly a Southern liberal believed blacks were biologically equal, and none would publicly speak out against racial segregation.

In the North, white liberalism had a presence. With the founding of the National Association for the Advancement of Colored People in 1909 and the National Urban League shortly thereafter, white liberalism reappeared.[9] Yet no one should overstate the racial liberalism of even the friends of the Negro in the North. Few outside of the new organizations dared to speak out against segregation as an institution in the South. Self-proclaimed Southern liberals, even those who advocated that liberal education should be afforded blacks, believed it best and proper for it to take place within the structure of segregation. Moreover, even in the North, white liberals were not agents of social change. In the North, the Young Men's Christian Association and the Young Women's Christian Association built separate facilities for black and white youth.[10] Virtually no one opposed the creation of the large ghettos. Finally, Julius Rosenwald, who underwrote black schools in the South and black housing projects in the North, would not hire African Americans to work in his corporation, Sears, Roebuck and Company.[11]

Among labor unions, even less racial liberalism existed. In the North, as well as the South, the American Federation of Labor allowed blacks to be discriminated against with impunity, ensuring that whites would enjoy a virtual monopoly on the skilled trades. As a result, African Americans had to establish segregated unions to have support.[12]

When Carter G. Woodson wrote in the wake of the Great War, this was the white audience to which he had to make his case for the Negro. It is no small wonder that his defense seems aimed at his black peers.

Fortunately, the Jim Crow gallery of 1921 was hardly a downtrodden crowd. The Great War and postwar optimism brought a new attitude to a large portion of the black community. With European immigration curtailed, African Americans had made headway in becoming part of the modern industrial workforce. Hundreds of thousands had migrated out of the rural South to the North, and many times more had left the countryside for Southern cities. Except at the borders, the expanding ghettos produced breathing space between blacks and whites and racial pride was everywhere in evidence. The "New Negro," as this generation of African Americans became known, was modern—urban, industrial, scientific, assertive, and increasingly proud of their heritage.[13]

In the arts and literature, African Americans dedicated themselves to producing creative expressions that proved the humanity and equality of black life. In Harlem and across the nation, a cultural awakening was taking place that would become known as the Harlem Renaissance. Du Bois had long hoped that African Americans would become recognized as "co-workers in the kingdom of culture," and this vision caught the spirit of the black intelligentsia. In music, art, and literature, the New Negro generation made itself known.

Without doubt the most dramatic expression of
the New Negro was Garveyism. Though centered in
Harlem, the Garvey Movement was stretched across
the continental United States wherever African Americans lived. In the South, Garvey had strongholds in
Florida, Georgia, and especially Louisiana. In the Midwest, Garveyism could be found in the major cities and
outposts like Omaha. On the West Coast, blacks in
Los Angeles fashioned a chapter that expressed their
new spirit as well. Historians have rightly noted the
importance of black communists, but we are coming
to understand that the reach of Garveyism went much
further into the fabric of black society, especially in
the South, the belly of the beast.[14]

Whites who sought to keep postwar blacks in
their place quickly discovered the presence of the New
Negro. Blacks met discrimination and rioting with
assertiveness. African Americans not only publicly
protested their treatment, they responded to violence
with self-defense. In places such as Chicago and Houston, the postwar riots resulted in the death of whites
as well as blacks.

Woodson was well aware of the spirit of the New
Negro, for he was part and parcel of it. In 1915, when
he established the Association for the Study of Negro
Life and History, it was born of the need he perceived
for African Americans to gain a greater appreciation

of their history and to defend the race against its traducers by countering falsehoods with facts. In 1921, Woodson incorporated The Associated Publishers so that deserving works related to black life and history would find their way into print and into the hands of African Americans and peoples of good will. He served as scholar and institution-builder, capitalist and philanthropist, mentor and employer, and servant to the race. Into his circle came future greats such as the poet Langston Hughes; the novelist and anthropologist Zora Neale Hurston; the artists James Lesesne Wells, James Porter, and Lois Mailou Jones; leaders such as Nannie Burroughs, John Hope, Mary McLeod Bethune, and Dorothy Height; and a phalanx of historians including Charles H. Wesley, Lorenzo Greene, Lawrence Reddick, and John Hope Franklin.

If anything, some New Negroes thought that Woodson's racial pride went too far. Beginning the intellectually flabby trend of having different definitions for black and white nationalism, Horace Mann Bond held that "in all fairness" Woodson and the Association were promoting a Negro nationalism "not necessarily inimical" to white nationalism. Undoubtedly influenced by Charles S. Johnson and E. Franklin Frazier, Gunnar Mrydal thought of Woodson as a racial chauvinist.[15]

Though not a nationalist—he never promoted African American self-governance or a return to Africa—Woodson was intensely ethnic. Woodson advocated black presidents for black institutions, refused to deal with white interracialists who had superiority complexes, and advocated black economic development. Except for the period of controversy surrounding Garvey's financial dealings, Woodson published a column in the United Negro Improvement Association (UNIA) for most of the 1920s. Woodson consorted with nationalists, along with Du Boisians, Washingtonians, communists, and the rising generation of integrationists.

No less than his *Mis-Education, Woodson's Appeal* provides grist for those who would like to misrepresent Woodson. Most of his major critics in the 1930s were still dependent on white philanthropy, and could gain or keep the favor of philanthropists by conflating criticism of white liberals with harboring anti-white or black nationalist politics. To be sure, in his *Appeal* Woodson spoke of whites who were "the enemies" and "detractors" of the race. That Woodson used such terms in projects that were written a decade apart make clear that even though Woodson was not a nationalist, he always stood in a defensive posture with his fists balled up ready to punch any and all who "traduced" his people. *Woodson's Appeal* epitomizes his lifelong defense of black people against all who opposed what he understood to be their best interest.

What is missing from *Woodson's Appeal* is any hint of criticism of the black middle class for being mis-educated. To the contrary, the black elite is represented as doing for the people—creating schools, establishing economic opportunity, and proper leadership. In short, black leadership is seen as progressive. As with Du Bois, who became disillusioned with the so-called talented tenth in the 1930s, Woodson's opinion changed with experience, turning negative by the late 1920s.

Woodson's optimism about black leadership centered on the development of the National Association for the Advancement of Colored People (NAACP). In Woodson's thinking, the NAACP stood in stark contrast to the race leadership that preceded it. Woodson speaks critically about what he called "indignation meetings," his derisive term for gatherings where members of the community come together to protest racist treatment at the hands of whites. In many of his later articles, there is insufficient discussion for properly gauging Woodson's thoughts on the contemporary debate between self-help versus protest, and it is easy to draw the erroneous conclusion that Woodson opposed protest activity. Some scholars, most notably the late August Meier, emphasized that Woodson was

sympathetic with Washington's approach to race relations. Others are perhaps too quick to dismiss any
comparison between the two, pointing to a couple of
anti-Washington statements made by Woodson over
the years. An understanding of Woodson's feelings
about "indignation meetings" sheds light on Woodson's views on protest and bootstraps.

Whatever he had in common with Washington,
Woodson's opposition was not to protesting injustice
but to a lack of organization and program. Indignation
meetings, in fact, were those that involved nothing
but expressions of racial outrage, "the empty protest
of the emotional element." In contrast were organized
efforts to address the cause of the outrage. Woodson even conceded that such meetings could lead to
more effective organization. Like a true Progressive,
Woodson wanted coordinated efforts and results. He
pointed to the example of Jews and Asians who were
despised and responded with the establishment of
newspapers to promote their cause. He took great
pride in the fact that "The Negro is too learning to use
proper methods to set his case before the world." Far
from opposing protest, he touted the creation of the
National Association for the Advancement of Colored
People, its 50,000 members, and its magazine, *The
Crisis,* that fought anti-black propaganda. He took
pride in the fact that blacks had progressed to the

point that "The orator without deeds, the promoter without a cause, the agitator without a desirable objective can no longer sway large masses of Negroes." Others might have disagreed with his assessment, but *Woodson's Appeal* evinces that Woodson was an advocate of programmatic protest.

Woodson's Appeal not only approves of developments in black political leadership, but also appears optimistic about black religious leaders. Students of African American history are well aware that educated blacks have had problems with black religious leaders stretching back to the 1830s when efforts were made to stamp out illiteracy among the ministers. For Woodson, ever a Progressive, the problem with black religion was not simply a lack of education among ministers but also a lack of social purpose. In his appeal Woodson boasted of the rise of the "institutional church," churches that created social programs to address the problems of their members and their community. He looked favorably on efforts to establish employment bureaus, gymnasiums, libraries, debating societies, and similar programs in the new institutional churches.

The NAACP and the institutional church represented the social justice dimension of the Progressive Era. Like all progressive initiatives, they sought to use modern scientific approaches to social change, and like most social justice reforms they sought to aid rather than blame the individual. In sum, what *Woodson's Appeal* of 1921 makes clear is that *The Mis-Education of the Negro* of 1933 is largely about the failure of black Progressivism.

If the black middle class is affirmed, the essay evinces that Woodson was ever in the corner of rank-and-file African Americans. Quite often he reversed the charges made against blacks and used them as proof of the shortcomings of the accusers. Woodson, for instance, took umbrage at the claim that black workers were shiftless and lazy. "The great trouble with these accusers," he wrote, is that "*they* rather than the Negroes need to learn to work." White men, he argued, often refused to do gainful employment and many of them listed by the census reports as laborers were actually cheating blacks of their money. "The trouble with so many white men today is that there are too many to live on the labor of a small number of Negroes." No wonder, he wrote, they accused blacks of being shiftless. Whites, held Woodson, had to learn that work was honorable, and he accused them of "unconsciously teach[ing] the white youth that it is dishonorable."

In his defense of African Americans and the black race more generally, Woodson often takes up the tactic of lodging the same charge against white Americans and comparing blacks favorably. In responding to the claim that blacks lack self-control and always indulge their sexual passions, Woodson points to illicit interracial sex that was almost always initiated by white men. "If the whites are so free from self-indulgence, how does it happen that more than one-fifth of the Negroes of the United States have an infusion of white blood?"

At times, Woodson would concede that blacks had shortcomings, but in most cases, he tended to blame slavery. In defense of the race's abilities, Woodson put forth an interpretation of colonial life that treated it as a veritable age of racial liberalism marred only by slavery. Prior to the advent of the cotton gin, people of African descent, he argued, were able to work their way out of slavery and become men of property and standing. Woodson provides examples of the descendants of slaves who had acquired enough land and slaves and white pigmentation that they could petition to be white. Some persons of color had even positioned themselves to hold whites as indentured servants. Summing the matter up, he wrote that "it has been estimated that more than 18,000 slaves were owned by Negroes during the period of slavery." As a doctorate holder in history from Harvard, Woodson was using his position as a specialist to put before the white readers information that white professors had not shared with them. In a world where the actual achievements of individuals were still used as evidence of racial worth, Woodson's research would have had shock value and thereby have forced some whites to rethink the capabilities of the Negro.

Much of what Woodson argued runs afoul of modern-day historical thinking and sensibilities. Historians debate whether the eighteenth century provided much opportunity for Africans to escape the thralldom of racism, if not institution of slavery. Yet there is a virtual consensus that the rise of the tobacco plantations in the early 1700s put an end to the opportunity structure for African Americans. Most of the individual Africans who would rise above slavery to become accepted on any level by whites had gained their freedom in the seventeenth century.

It goes without saying that Woodson's use of slaveholding as evidence of black equality is a perverse argument. A few years after he wrote "The Case of the Negro," Woodson defended most black slaveholding as familial and philanthropic. Since then, many scholars who emphasize class suggest that he was much too generous in interpreting the motives of the slaveholders of color. In citing the slaveholding evidence, he was certainly not in the business of seeking to demonstrate that blacks, as a group, were equally capable of oppression.

To the contrary, Woodson believed that the experience of blacks, especially here in America, had made them different from whites. In the mid-1950s, Kenneth Stampp, the liberal historian of slavery, ran afoul of the 1960s generation by stating that blacks were merely white men in black skins.[16] As if in response to Stampp, Woodson remarked, "The Negro is not a white man in a black skin." Momentarily forgetting that he was presenting the case *for* the Negro, Woodson wrote, "If the blacks were suddenly transformed in spirit into white people the racial conflict...would give rise to a state of anarchy." Painting a picture of a war in which evil would be pitted against evil, he writes that developments "would not only drench the soil with blood but would result in the extermination of a large portion of mankind."

In Woodson's hands, discussions of race, culture, politics, and religion all had a way of becoming a critique of white Americans. Woodson's tact on dealing with the racial makeup of the Negro was to cast doubt on the whole question of race. In doing this, he simply joined a whole line of black intellectuals from the antebellum period until his own age. Yet as was his wont, Woodson was decidedly different. Whereas most black intellectuals sought to validate the racial stock of people of African descent, Woodson defended blacks by antagonizing whites, poking at their racial preten-

sions. Rather than simply saying that racial theories
were increasingly questionable in light of recent scientific advances, a view that was leading experts to doubt
that there was any such thing as pure races, Woodson
took his pen and burst the white balloon. "The average
Caucasian," he wrote, "is no nearer the representative
of a single type and in many cases no nearer to the
actual white man than many so-called Negroes." For
Woodson, whites deviated from purity because their
racial origin was not Aryan, as was once supposed,
but African. Southern Europeans and Teutons alike,
he argued, were a Eura-African racial stock, "a brown
Mediterranean race."

Along with taking shots at the racial arrogance of
whites, Woodson took aim to reduce whites a notch or
two in their understanding of themselves as the cre-
ators of civilization based on Christianity and democracy. Woodson took pains to argue that black people
were more religious and better Christians than the
whites who criticized their relationship to religion.
"The blacks," he writes, "are superior to whites in that
they are more religious." After examining the barbarous history of whites in their dealings with the rest
of the world, he states, "The Negro, therefore, has
little faith in the so-called Christian civilization. He is
not inclined to ascribe to this religion in its corrupted
form credit which it has received as the supreme and

absolute in bringing the world to its present advanced stage." Emphasizing that blacks were Christians who believed in the principles of Jesus, he held that "The Negro agrees with that writer who says that whites nailed Christianity to the cross. There is much doubt that actual Christianity ever existed in Europe and even if it did, it suffered an untimely death in transit across the Atlantic."

Woodson's view of America's party system equaled his assessment of white Christianity. American policies, he argued, were set "by inconsiderate and narrow-minded prejudiced charlatans like William Howard Taft and Woodrow Wilson, who have no desire to rule justly but merely endeavor to serve efficiently the machines by which they are controlled." He held that the political parties that ran America were "jealous," "clannish," and "autocratic." On the world stage, as well as at home, Wilson, according to Woodson, aimed to serve white interests. Wilson's brainchild, the League of Nations, was merely "a compact to organize all of the powerful nations selfishly interested in their own welfare as was proved by the attitude of the Peace Conference in refusing to grant the request of Japan to eliminate race prejudice." Despite the shortcomings of America's white leadership, Woodson held that blacks loved their country. Given these views, it is no small wonder that Lorenzo

Greene, Woodson's protege at the Association, would later suggest that his mentor was ambivalent in his American patriotism.[17]

One can only imagine how Woodson's words would have been received had he published them in 1922. His critique of both the Republican and Democratic parties, his harsh remarks about racial liberals and white Christianity may very well have proven counterproductive for a black man on a mission to build an organization strong enough to change the image of an oppressed race. The same year, The Laura Spelman Rockefeller Memorial Fund and the Carnegie Foundation awarded ASNLH major grants that allowed him to cease teaching, undertake research through the Association, purchase the now famous 9th Street address, and invest in a publishing house. The grants paid him $4,000 a year for five years, a sum of roughly $50,000 a year in today's dollars. Frugal and shrewd, Woodson decided to lay low.[18]

In an age when white philanthropy and liberal opinion determined so much of what black leaders and intellectuals said and did, Woodson would shortly become one of the truly independent intellectuals of his era. The relationship among his personal finances, the Association's dealings, and his publishing house were such that the Internal Revenue Service and Woodson were ongoing correspondents. The year following the end of the grant period, Woodson owned the 9th Street property free and clear. In effect, it had been paid for in part through the grant indirectly as the Association's rent. The other portion was paid for through the rent paid by The Associated Publishers. The IRS apparently accepted his claim that he was allowed free housing by his two employers in the dwelling that he rented to them. (Indeed, he insisted he was a resident of West Virginia!) Initially during the Great Depression, his income dipped to as low as $1,800 a year, but rebounded to the $2,400 range during the early 1930s. During the depression, he often refused a salary (though not the rent) from the Association. With his housing costs paid, he could easily survive on a modest salary.[19]

The Association laid the silver eggs that drove the profits of The Associated Publishers. The research funds from grants produced many of the manuscripts that provided the revenue for his for-profit company. The Association, rather than Woodson or The Associated Publishers, paid for his travels that resulted in publications. The Association's promotion of Negro History Week created a market for The Associated Publishers' Negro History Week products. While Woodson never sought to create an exceedingly profitable publishing house, it should be recognized that The Associated Publishers remained a viable business with

an expanding list of titles for the nearly thirty years
that Woodson ran it. It paid Woodson the landlord
several hundred dollars a month in rent on a debt-
free building and Woodson the executive a salary of
$1,200 a year.[20]

Once financially situated, Woodson resumed his
tendency of running afoul of the white, liberal establishment and the black folks in their court. On the
dime of the association that he built and controlled,
Woodson traveled to Europe, especially Paris, for
several summers during the Great Depression, carrying forward his scholarly agenda and renewing his
spirit. He was free to criticize leading whites and leading blacks, friends and foes, liberals and conserva-
tives, presidents and supremacists and combinations
thereof.[21] By the late 1920s, Woodson had become too
troublesome for the foundations to fund any further,
but what a fortified position he had constructed out of
the monies made available to him! He never aspired to
be or became rich, but he had used white folks' money
to secure his intellectual freedom and independence.

In contrast, Du Bois never obtained financial independence. During the Great Depression, Du Bois
concluded that blacks needed to congregate and form
cooperatives. Black leaders joined white liberals in calling Du Bois a "self-segregationist," and stripped him
of his editorship of *The Crisis* and put him in need of

employment. Du Bois found it necessary to return to Atlanta University and remain on his best behavior lest he jeopardize the institution.[22] After the passing of his friend John Hope, the university's president, Du Bois found himself vulnerable and was eventually released.

The contrasting financial situation is best seen in their responses to philanthropy in the matter of the infamous encyclopedia project. From the early to mid-1930s, the Phelps-Stokes foundation flirted with the idea of moving forward with a black encyclopedia, attempting to do so without either Du Bois or Woodson. Along with being the first and second African Americans with doctorates in history from Harvard, both had plans for such an encyclopedia, and Woodson had already begun research on his. Because some black intellectuals understood that the project would lack legitimacy without them, they were approached. After being named the editor of the project, Du Bois urged Woodson to go along with their program. Exercising his hard-earned intellectual freedom, Woodson refused and gave all involved a piece of his mind. Of Du Bois's decision to participate, he wrote that "poverty makes strange bedfellows." He did not expect the whites organizing the project to contact him, he wrote, "for they know well that I have the greatest contempt for them, and that I do not want any of their money or any funds which they can raise."[23]

In the decades since the federal government crushed Black Power radicalism, we hear much from intellectuals who "speak truth to power." It is one of the favorite sayings of the self-styled radicals of our day. Yet it appears that Woodson understood that you don't *always* say all that is on your mind, and perhaps there are truths that should not be spoken—at least not without due consideration. Sometimes truth should be spoken in whispers as one organizes and plans behind Power's back—after all, Power *is* powerful. That's what prudent people and successful revolutionaries tend to do. Woodson, of course, was no revolutionary, simply a man who knew how to bide his time and how to build an institution that could survive the caprice of philanthropy. We are now fortunate to know just what The Father of Black History was thinking as he built a business and an Association that underwrote his intellectual freedom and independence.

Daryl Michael Scott
Howard University

Notes

1 *David Walker's Appeal: To the Coloured Citizens of the World,* with an Introduction by James Turner. (Baltimore: Black Classics Press, 1993); W. E. B. Du Bois, *The Souls of Black Folk* (Chicago: A. C. McClurg, 1903).

2 E. Franklin Frazier, *The Black Bourgeoisie,* (New York: The Free Press, 1997); and Harold Cruse, *The Crisis of the Negro Intellectual,* (New York: New York Review of Books, 2005).

3 Du Bois as quoted in Jacqueline Goggin, *Carter G. Woodson: A Life in Black History* (Baton Rouge: Louisiana State University Press, 1993), 181.

4 Carter G. Woodson, *The Mis-Education of the Negro,* edited by Daryl Michael Scott, foreward by V.P. Franklin (Washington: The ASALH Press, 2005).

5 There appears to have been very little positive contact between Woodson and Du Bois. Besides the debate over the encyclopedia, Woodson believed that Du Bois, along with Kelly Miller, gave his effort to establish the Association little chance for success. See Woodson, "The Meagre Contribution to Leadership in Washington," *Boston Chronicle,* (n.d., 1933).

6 W. J. Cash, *The Mind of the South* (New York: Vintage Books, 1991).

7 William Tuttle, *Race Riot: Chicago in the Red Summer of 1919* (New York: Atheneum, 1970).

8 See Kenneth T. Jackson, *The Ku Klux Klan in the City, 1915-1930* (New York: Oxford, 1967).

9 Charles Flint Kellogg, *NAACP: A History of the National Association for the Advancement of Colored People,* Vol. 1, 1909–1920 (Baltimore: Johns Hopkins University Press, 1967); Arvarh E. Strickland, *History of the Chicago Urban League* (Urbana: University of Illinois Press, 1966); and Guichard Parris and Lester Brooks, *Black in the Cities: A History of the National Urban League* (Boston: Little & Brown, 1971).

10 For a history of African Americans and the YMCA move-
ment in America, see Nina Mjagkij, *Light in the Darkness:
African Americans and the YMCA, 1852-1946* (Lexington,
KY: University Press of Kentucky, 1994).

11 Rosenwald's philanthropy has received much deserved at-
tention, but virtually no attention is given his exclusion of
African Americans from significant employment at Sears and
Roebuck. For the most recent biography of the trend-setting
philanthropist, see Peter M. Ascoli, *Julius Rosenwald: The
Man Who Built Sears, Roebuck and Advanced the Cause
of Black Education in the American South* (Bloomington:
Indiana University Press, 2006).

12 The literature of African Americans and unions is volumi-
nous. See Ernest Obadele-Starks provides an outstanding
example of the organization of black labor unions in the
South in *Black Unionism in the Industrial South* (College
Station, Texas: Texas A.M. University Press, 1999); also see
Beth Bates, *Pullman Porters and the Rise of Protest Politics
in Black America, 1925-1945* (University of North Carolina
Press, 2001); and Eric Arneson, *Waterfront Workers of New
Orleans* (Urbana: University of Illinois Press, 1863-1923).

13 Alain Locke, "Enter the New Negro," *Survey Graphic*, March
1925.

14 Important studies on the Garvey movement include: Tony
Martin, *Race First* (Westport, Conn.: Greenwood Press,
1976); Emory Tolbert, *The UNIA and Black Los Angeles :
Ideology and Community in the American Garvey Movement*
(Los Angeles: Center for Afro-American Studies, 1980); and
Judith Stein, *The World of Marcus Garvey* (Baton Rouge:
Louisiana State University Press, 1986). For years scholars
have glimpsed the importance of the Garvey movement in
the American South. For a useful treatment see, Mary G.
Rolinson, *Grassroots Garveyism* (Chapel Hill: University of
North Carolina Press, 2007).

15 Horace Mann Bond, "The Curriculum and the Negro Child,"
Journal of Negro Education 4 (April 1935), 163. To get the

gist of Bond's sentiments toward Woodson, one should con-
sult his review of Woodson's *Mis-Education of the Negro* in
which he compares Woodson to William Hannibal Thomas, a
racial critic consumed by self-hate. In a few short years, Bond
would find Woodson's alleged nationalist tendencies useful
when he was in need of a publisher for *Negro Education in
Alabama: A Study in Cotton and Steel* (Washington, DC:
Associated Publishers, 1939); see "Dr. Woodson goes Wool
Gathering," *Journal of Negro Education* 2 (April 1933), 210-
213; Gunnar Myrdal, *An American Dilemma* (New York:
Harper & Row, 1944), 752.

16 Kenneth Stampp, *The Peculiar Institution,* (New York:
Vintage Books, 1956), vii-viii.

17 Lorenzo Greene, *Working with Carter G. Woodson, the
Father of Black History, 1928-1930* (Baton Rouge: Louisiana
State University Press, 1989), 454.

18 The inflation calculator is based on the consumer index taken
since 1913, and can be found at the website of the regional
federal reserve: http://minneapolisfed.org/research/data/us/
calc/; C.G. Woodson, Internal Revenue Service Form 1040A,
1925.

19 C. G. Woodson to T. M. B. Dunn of IRS, dated September
11, 1924; Galen L. Tait of IRS to Carter G. Woodson, dated
January 15, 1927; C. G. Woodson to A. J. Trageser, dated
January 17, 1927; Galen E. Tait to Carter G. Woodson,
November 20, 1930; Carter G. Woodson to A. J. Trageser,
November 14, 1930; C. G. Woodson to A. J. Trageser, dated
November 21, 1930; C. G. Woodson to A. J. Trageser, dated
November 29, 1930; C. G. Woodson, Internal Revenue Service
Form 1040A for years 1929 through 1934. "History Group
Reflects Officers; Insist Salary Be Paid Carter Woodson," St.
Louis *Argus* (September 20, 1940).

20 In letters written but never sent to the Internal Revenue
Service in 1940, Woodson still listed his salaries from ASNLH
and the Associated Publishers as $100.00 a month each, re-
spectively. C. G. Woodson, head of the Associated Publishers,

to IRS, November 15, 1940, and C. G. Woodson, Director of ASNLH, to IRS, November 15, 1940.

21 Woodson's travels to Paris were frequent. In 1943, Woodson wrote of being in Paris with the author J. A. Rogers in 1932. The next year, Woodson traveled to Spain in late January. In his annual report for 1935, he stated that he was spending three months annually in Europe, suggesting that he was probably there in 1934 as well. In 1937, Woodson saw Lois Mailou Jones off to Paris, and during her yearlong stay, he dined with her while there. See Carter G. Woodson, A Review of *Sex and Race* (New York, 1943) *Journal of Negro History* 28 (January 1943), 91-92; Baltimore *The Afro-American* (January 28, 1933); An Interview with Lois Mailou Jones, by Charles H. Rowell *Callaloo*, Vol. 12 No. 2, p. 357-378; Carter G. Woodson, "Annual Report of the Director," *Journal of Negro History* 20 (October 1935), 365.

22 Du Bois faced being silenced or leaving the editorship of *The Crisis*. Kenneth Robert Janken, *White: The Biography of Walter White, Mr. NAACP* (New York: The New Press, 2003), 190-191. The role of the Atlanta University trustees in his hiring is discussed by David Levering Lewis, *W. E. B. Du Bois: The Fight for Equality and the American Century, 1919-1963* (New York: Holt, 2000), 316-317. Still thinking as a product of the age of philanthropy, Du Bois would later chide foundations for not supporting Woodson's work and forcing him, according to Du Bois's estimate, to live in poverty. W. E. B. Du Bois, "The White Folk Have a Right to Be Ashamed," *The National Guardian* 17 (February 7, 1949), 6-7.

23 C. G. Woodson, "An Open Letter to the *Afro-American* on the Negro Encyclopedia," Press Release, June 3, 1936; and C. G. Woodson, "Remember 1917," Press Release, June 17, 1936. Carter G. Woodson Papers, Library of Congress.

1

What the Negro Is

Exactly what the Negro is in the anthropological sense is no more a perplexing question than the racial origin of the so-called white man. The average Caucasian is no nearer the representative of a single type and in many cases no nearer to the actual white man than many so-called Negroes. According to William Z. Ripley there is no single European white race of men and we may well conclude from the results of long contact of the whites with the blacks in America that this is still less true on this side of the Atlantic.[1] Science has uprooted the idea of Asia as the home of the Aryan from whom came cultural descendants who brought into Europe the Greek, Roman, and Teutonic civilizations and there is a tendency toward increasing doubt as to many other theories concerning racial groups still accepted by a few writers.

The classification of members of the human family has not yet been productive of valuable information. By measuring the heads of the mummies found in Egypt a certain anthropologist decided that the ancient Egyptians belonged to the white race. Another man classified black Abyssinians as whites. These things, however, mean little when scientists have shown that the European race itself is of secondary origin, that the earliest and lowest population of Europe were an extremely long-headed type of the stone age and that after the partial occupation of western Europe by a dolichocephalic Africanoid type in the stone age, an invasion by a broad-headed race from Asia followed.

Guiseppi Sergi believes that the migration of the African racial element took place in primitive times from north to south and that types of Cro-Magnon, L'homme-Mort and other French and Belgian localities bear witness to the presence of African stock in the same region in which we find the dolmens and other megalithic monuments erroneously attributed to the Celts.[2] What must we say then of Sergi's conclusions that as a result of this movement of peoples northward out of Africa that the primitive population of the Mediterranean originated in Africa, that from this Eura-African stock came the present inhabitants of North Africa, the southern European stock and Teuton, and that this primitive people was one of color, a brown Mediterranean race? It is highly probable then that the Paleolithic man of Europe was not essentially different from the Protonigritian of Australia who has remained in his undeveloped state because he was cut off from the rest of the world by geological changes in the crust of the earth.[3]

In America the study of the races has been biased. The fruitless effort to prove the inferiority of the Negro before the Civil War by taking physiological differences as a basis has led to all sorts of conclusions such as to separate origin of various races even so ludicrous as the non-sense that dark races are the descendants of incestuous intercourse between man and monkey. Men of scholarship, however, think only of the origin of the human race as monogenetic. No scientist considers the human race as divided into five groups. Dr. Felix von Luschan says that "the question of the number of human races has quite lost its raison d'etre and has become a subject rather of philosophical speculation than of scientific research. It is of no more importance now to know how many human races there are than to know how many angels can stand on the point of a needle." The aim of the investigator, he believes, "is to find how ancient and primitive races developed from others, and how races have changed or evolved through migration and interbreeding."[4] Neither all black men nor all white men belong to the same race. It is contended that the Africans, for example, differ anatomically from the Australian blacks, as the former with the exception of the superior Hamites who figured in making the civilization of Egypt, Abyssinia, Housa, Galla-Somal and Masailand, developed into real Negroes produced in sequestered parts of Africa by climatic conditions.

Writers have also made the mistake of attaching civilization to color. In the geographies of prejudiced America one still finds the illustration of the well-dressed and intelligent-looking white man to represent the Caucasian race whereas the Negro is represented by a black woolly-haired, flat nose bushman portrayed as a brute seeking what he may devour. The usual aim is to set before the youth an ideal of beauty which tradition has attached to physiological characteristics and to portray it as the representative of a superior white man's civilization. The ideas of ugliness or beauty, of savagery or civilization, however, are purely relative terms. The natives of Africa regard nothing white as attractive, and see beauty only in the black. The Negroes in the United States with the white man's conception of beauty, quickly absorb the mulatto offspring of lustful white men and thousands of Negroes spend much of their earnings for cosmetics and hair growing preparations to meet the requirements of this ideal group. The European is easily attracted by the slender fashionable woman of symmetric physique, the Persian highly prizes the corpulent woman approaching nearer to the Amazonian and the Japanese find horrid the large eyes and high noses of the whites.

We often misuse the term civilized people when judging men in our own standard. Primitive races whom we consider underdeveloped surpass us in certain respects in which we are supposed to be their superiors. White people boast of their cleanliness but a man is supposed to meet the requirements when he bathes twice a week and many of them do not bathe more than once a week while millions never use a tooth brush. Most of the belated races bathe daily and it is said that the Bantu and other African peoples clean their teeth after every meal. Referring to dress Dr. Felix von Luschan says that the primitive man can have a highly developed sense of modesty though naked, whereas civilized people observe much immodesty in silk and velvet. "Primitive people are analphabets but," says he, "so are ninety percent of the Russians; but the primitive people have stronger memory which deteriorates with the invention of writing."[5]

That all races are not equally advanced no one will doubt. Such differences as environment, exceptional circumstances, and commercial advantages have brought it to pass that some branches of the human stock have outstripped the others but whether the races be white or black, apparently like or unlike, primitive or modern, they are all from a common source. Give all races the belated opportunities enjoyed by the more advanced and history shows that in the end there will be little difference in achievement. The Japanese were considered a backward, primitive people until the middle of the last century but now they have superiors neither among the living nor the dead.

The question of racial inferiority easily exposes its own fallacy. For example, a farmer has two sons. The one meets with better opportunities than the other in that he fortunately casts his lot in an environment where he can earn more and is encouraged to do more than his brother does elsewhere. The more favorably circumstanced youth develops into a man of education and wealth whereas his brother does not rise above the status of his impecunious father. Must we, therefore, conclude that the fortunate brother is superior to the other? Could not the less fortunate youth have made a more successful man of himself, if he had been similarly circumstanced? Why then should we think of the Negro as an inferior to the white man merely because the latter has had a better chance? Is the Indian inferior to the Negro because the former has perished before the onward sweep of western civilization? Is the Russian serf inferior to the German because he is mentally underdeveloped and unduly primitive? Were the Greeks inferior to the Mesopotamians because the latter were first to show decided advancement in culture? No seeker of the truth will waste time with such fallacies.

There has been an effort also to prove the inferiority of the Negro by showing racial variations with respect to the weight of the frontal lobe and the like. It has been contended that there is variation of the germ of splenium of the corpus callosum due to race, that the frontal lobe of the Negro brain is lighter than that of the whites. Believing too that the brains of men of genius are of complex configuration, writers like A. J. Parker have endeavored to show that the fissures of the Negro brain are shorter since they approach those of the monkey or are more foetal in character. By investigation conducted in the anatomical laboratory of Johns Hopkins using the same instruments as well as the same brains as several of the writers who reached these adverse conclusions, Franklin P. Mall has compared the results from the investigation of the brains of Negroes along with whites without regard to race. It turns out that the so-called anatomical differences as to the richness of the brains in gyri and sulci which were once thought to indicate intellectual power mean nothing. [6] Such differences may be found also in the brains of Negroes which defeats the purpose of the biased investigation. In fact, it has been shown that when jumbled together the scientist cannot by investigation distinguish the brains of whites from those of blacks.

Tests as to the sense of hearing, smell, touch, color and speed in mental and motor performances have generally broken down. No two individuals are alike. If two such persons could be found, nature could get along just as well without one of them. No one, therefore, can represent a race. Furthermore, the effort to obtain an average for a certain group has proved to be ludicrous for the average does not indicate the amount of variation within the group and the range of variation within the group is generally greater than the difference between the averages of the groups. For example, while one investigator shows the brain of Negroes average two ounces lighter than that of Europeans, the range of variation within either race amounts to twenty-five ounces. It has been discovered too that though races slightly differ on average in color and hair they overlap each other so much that with the exception of language and superficial mannerisms obtaining the average is not worth while.

Statements to the effect that certain races lack powers of reasoning, memory, perception, abstraction, inhibition or foresight are also without scientific foun-dation. No race has yet proved its exclusive monopoly of mental power. If so, the lowest grade of intelligence among the whites would be higher than the lowest grade among the blacks; but as a matter of fact the one descends to as low a level as the other. Differences in culture do not prove mental traits. Woodworth discovered that when individuals composing a race are tested, those who rank high in one trait do not always rank high in others.[7] A group may be so circumstanced as not to have an opportunity for the development of certain mental powers whereas another may have the proper environment. Because a nation may be more advanced than another is no more an argument for its superior mental power than the argument that a nation in its advanced stage has more mental endowment than when undeveloped. Scientists contend that advancement is a cumulative process not a result of increasing mental power or a biological modification of the brain.

Many pseudo-scientists used to say that the Negro approaches nearer to the primitive man in that he is carried away like a child by impulse of the environment and that he is incapable of self-restraint, incapable of rejecting immediate gratification for a greater future one. To prove the absurdity of this Professor William I. Thomas of the University of Chicago has undertaken to show that since restraints exercised in a group depend largely on tradition as to views and objects, these conclusions have no scientific foundation. He refers to the fact that in the great majority of

American Indian and Australian tribes a man is strictly forbidden to kill or eat the animal whose name his clan bears as a totem. The central Australian may not under certain conditions eat flesh of any animal which has been touched by persons standing in certain relations of kinship to him. At certain times he is forbidden to eat the flesh of a number of animals and at all times he must share all food secured with the tribal elders and some others. Continuing this discussion further he says, "A native of Queensland will put his mark on an unripe zamia and may be sure it will be untouched and that when it is ripe he has only to go and get it. The Eskimo though starving will not molest the sacred seal basking before his hut. The west African fetish acts as a police and property protected by it is safer than under civilized laws. Food and palm wine are placed beside the path a piece of fetish suspended nearby and no one will touch them without leaving the proper payment. The garden of a native may be a mile from the house, unfenced and sometimes unvisited for weeks by the owner; but it is immune from depredation if protected by fetish."[8] This does not look very much like a lack of restraint among the primitive people.

This power of abstraction has been pointed out as another basis of difference. Persons who have not yet obtained sufficient power of abstraction to be able to distinguish between the ability to think in the ab-

stract and the ability to think otherwise have said that
the undeveloped races lack the power of abstraction.
When this is properly analyzed it turns out that the
differences observed are due largely to environment
which in the case of the modern nations has been decidedly multiplied by science, philosophy, and logic
estimates of reckoning time, space and number. As
the native is not engaged in perceptual deliberate acts
there is not any need for the development of the power
of thinking in the abstract. Further investigations show
that all peoples possess this power to some extent, and
that they do not suffer in comparison when they have
been submitted to a fair test.

Professor William I. Thomas of the University of
Chicago believes that the proverb, a form of abstraction practiced by all races, is perhaps the best test
of abstraction. Taking this as a standard one must
conclude that the natives of Africa with their large
store house of sentient expressions equal to those of
the most civilized nations on the globe must possess
the power of abstraction to a very great extent. "If the
activities are simple," says Professor Thomas, "the
mind is simple and if the activities are nil the mind
will be nil. The mind is nothing but a means of ma-
nipulating the outside world. Number, time and space
conceptions and estimates become more complex and
inaccurate, not as the human mind grows in capac-

ity but as activities become more varied and call for more extended and accurate systems of notation and measurement. Trade and commerce, machinery and manufacture and all the processes of civilization involve specialization in the apprehension of series as such. Under these conditions the number technique becomes elaborate and requires time and instruction for its master."[9]

As to morals it is very clear that most of these primitive people are not inferior to persons considered much more advanced. It has been reported that the patterns of morality found among the African Kaffirs are very much like those of the Hebrews. The Kaffirs are said to enact laws which meet every crime which may be committed. They punish theft by restitution and fine; injured cattle by death or fine; false witness by fine; adultery by fine or death; poisoning or witchcraft by death and forfeiture of property; murder by death or fine; treason or desertion from the tribe by death and confiscation. Polygamy among primitive peoples is general but every woman is attached to some man. The lewd woman common among Americans and Europeans, therefore, has no place among the belated races. Such evils as drunkenness and venereal diseases and tuberculosis were not known to rage among the savages until they came into contact with Christians.

If we face complexities when we endeavor to determine exactly what the Europeans are, what shall we expect of the mongrel American whites and especially of the Negroes who in the census reports include all classes and numbers not wanted by the white race although the infusion of Negro blood is decidedly small. Considered anthropologically the name Negro does not mean much and the color line breaks down scientifically when scientists have shown that the man with a dark skin, wooly hair, thick lips and flat nose turns out in many cases to be anatomically like unto the white man in other characteristics. This results from a lack of pigment in the north where because of climatic conditions it is not needed, for color according to scientists is a physiological difference to climate, the rays of the sun and humidity. The difference of hair is that the wooly hair is flat whereas the straight is round.

Of his peculiar basis of classification, however, Theodor Waitz has concluded that the Gallas, Nubians, Hottentots, the natives of the Congo and the Malagasies, the Shillooks and Bongoes are not genuine Negroes. Now if we add to these the light colored natives of South Africa and the Kaffirs who are also regarded as non-members of the Negro race, one must inquire where shall Negroes be found?[10] They are apparently scarce in Africa and even where explorers find Negroes in Africa they discover many other mixed breeds. What then shall we say of the Negroes of the United States one-fifth of whom are mulattoes? What must be the conclusion regarding the whites of the United States where thousands of apparently white Negroes annually cross the line into the ranks of their self-styled superiors who never have reason to question them on account of their color.

These facts bring us to the inevitable conclusion that the history of the human race is unknown. The blind unscientific investigators who are generalizing on certain observations of a few members of a group of persons of color, therefore, are not misinforming the intelligent people of the day, for any enlightened man can understand that the facts thus obtained may be from members of widely differing races. We can easily prove that neither Booker T. Washington nor Frederick Douglass was white but no one can prove that they belonged to the same stock. Arabs, Hindus, Portugese and Greeks are known in certain parts as colored people.

Notes

1 William Zebina Ripley, *The Races of Europe: A Sociological Study* (D. Appleton, 1910).

2 In 1911 and again in 1916, W. E. B. Du Bois published an essay in which he cited Italian Anthropologist Guiseppi Sergi's view that African racial stock had migrated to Europe, a theory too delicious for either Woodson or him to pass up. A true racial liberal, Sergi position was that Germans and Scandinavians were of African racial stock rather than Aryan. "They are Eurafrican of the Nordic variety." The idea that the European dolmens, or stone tombs with massive capstones, were the proof of an African presence flew in the face of received knowledge and appears to have never taken hold in scientific or popular circles. William E. Burghart Du Bois, "Races of Men," in *Select Discussions of Race Problems*, edited by J. A. Bingham, *The Atlanta University Publications*, No. 20. (Atlanta: The Atlanta University Press, 1916), 19; Guiseppi Sergi, *The Mediterranean Race: A Study of the Origin of European Peoples* (New York: Charles Scribner's Sons, 1901), vi-vii, 70.

3 Felix von Luschan, "Anthropological View of Race," in *Select Discussions of Race Problems*, edited by J. A. Bingham, *The Atlanta University Publications*, No. 20. (Atlanta: The Atlanta University Press, 1916), 27.

4 Ibid., 26, 47.

5 Ibid., 25.

6 It appears that Woodson drew this material from Franklin P. Mall, who delivered a paper "On Several Anatomical Characters of the Human Brain Said to Vary According to Race and Sex, with Especial Reference to the Weight of the Frontal Lobe," at the last of the Atlanta University conferences led by. W. E. B. Du Bois in 1915. See *Select Discussions of Race Problems*, edited by J. A. Bingham, *The Atlanta University Publications*, No. 20. (Atlanta: The Atlanta University Press, 1916), 47. Franklin P. Mall (1862-1917) taught at Johns

Hopkins medical school from 1893 until his death, serving as the first professor of anatomy. Woodson may very well have known of his article from a different source, for it appears that Mall was invited to the conference to present the work, for it had been published several years earlier under the same title in *American Journal of Anatomy* 9: 1-32 (1909). For more information on Mall, see, http://www.medicalarchives.jhmi.edu/sgml/mall.html as retrieved on Oct. 29, 2006 18:19:55 GMT. The essay became quite important for black social scientists keeping track with what experts had to say about race. See Charles S. Johnson and Horace M. Bond, "Investigation of Racial Differences Prior to 1910," *Journal of Negro Education* 1934 (331). The major study to which Mall was responding is A. J. PARKER, Cerebral Convolutions of the Negro-Brain. *Proceedings of the Academy of Natural Sciences of Philadelphia for the year 1878*. S. 11. — (Philadelphia, 1879), 8.

7 R. S. Woodworth, "Racial Differences in Mental Traits." Science 1910 31 (788), 171-186. Paul F. Ballantyne, "Robert S. Woodworth (1869-1962): Career Overview and Contemporary Significance," http://www.comnet.ca/~pballan/Woodworth. htm as retrieved on Oct. 27, 2006 05:25:22 GMT; See also, R. S. Woodworth, "Robert S. Woodworth," in C. Murchison (Ed.)., *A History of Psychology in Autobiography* Vol. 2 (Worcester, MA: Clark University Press, 1930), 359-380..

8 William I. Thomas, "The Mind of the Savage," in *Select Discussions of Race Problems*, edited by J. A. Bingham, *The Atlanta University Publications*, No. 20 (Atlanta: The Atlanta University Press, 1916), 77.

9 Ibid., 79.

10 Woodson's reference to Waitz appears to be based on Du Bois's essay "Races of Men," not simply Waitz. Woodson discusses the "Bangoes," who do not appear in Waitz's book, but appears in Du Bois's essay. Du Bois also relies on Waitz to make the point that modern authorities now looked at Africans as representing numerous racial groups, Negroes be-

ing only one and then a small fraction. Above, Woodson attributes to Waitz the notion that the Bongoes and Shillooks were not Negroes, but Du Bois attributes that view to Schweinfurth. In the third edition of *Heart of Africa*, published in 1878, Georg Schweinfurth referred to Shillooks as Negroes, and as one of the "negro races." Vol. I, (London: Sampson Low Marston, Searle & Riventon, 1878), 19. In Waitz's 1863 textbook, no mention is made of the Bangos or Bongoes, and "the Shillook" are treated like a non-Negro race. Theodor Waitz, "Introduction to Anthropology," edited by J. Frederick Collingwood, (London: Longman, 1863), 211. It appears that Du Bois and Woodson gave imprecise attributions of their views. Whatever the source of confusion, both Woodson and Du Bois were struck by the view that various racial groups inhabited Africa, not just Negroes. For Du Bois's view see *Select Discussions of Race Problems*, edited by J. A. Bingham, *The Atlanta University Publications, No. 20* (Atlanta: The Atlanta University Press, 1916), 21.

2

What the Negro Has Done

In spite of all that we may say about what the Negro is, the people living in the same community with members of this race know much less about them than they know about most groups around them. The very color and status of the Negro, in a society in which he is debased to the plane of the proletariat unworthy of civic and political privileges, makes him such a repellent force that the race has never been an object of scientific study. Most men usually dispose of the thought of studying the Negro very much as a planter in the South, when in reply to an appeal for a subscription to a Negro publication on the ground that the world should know more about the race, responded that he had been among Negroes all of his life and that he knew a great deal more about them than he wanted to know. The fact is that even in the South where the contact of the races may be supposed to be extensive, the one knows very little about the other save to the extent of the information obtained through occasional contact. The majority of the white people of the South know the Negroes only through the servants attached to their homes. As the servant class has in the development of the race gradually lost the ambitious and progressive blacks, this element constitutes now only the weakest members of the group. This class is decidedly unrepresentative of the actual character of the race and does not indicate the stage of civilization which it has attained.

Even if it can be contended that the white man's knowledge of the Negro in America is adequate to make a just estimate of the worth of the race, few men will gainsay the contention that the so-called civilized portion of the world still knows very little of what is going on in Africa and the historic background of the Negroes on that continent. Until students of ethnology, history, and philosophy engage in an intensive study of the institutions of the peoples of the interior of Africa, it will be impossible for modern scholarship to make any authoritative evaluation of African culture. A few writers, like A. B. Ellis, Felix Dubois, and others, have by their limited investigation sufficiently penetrated the large unexplored archives of African history to convince the world by their research indicative of more extensive results that Africa is still an unknown land.[1]

History shows that the primitive peoples of Africa did not differ materially from the primitive peoples of Europe or Asia. They passed through the family stage to that of the clan, then to a tribal state, and finally emerged as the builders of great empires, the ruins of which may be still observed. When civilization moved westward it spread into Africa as well as into Europe. In Egypt, among Negroid people, who in this country would be hissed and jeered as blacks, it reached a greater height than the culture of the world had experienced prior to the development of the Greek civilization. At no time did the Negroes fail to figure conspicuously in the civilization of Egypt, as is evidenced by the fact that full-blooded Negroes like Ra Nehesi and Nefertari sat on the Egyptian throne, and that many other of its rulers were of decidedly Negroid features. And it was not confined merely to the northern part of Africa. We know very much about Egypt because of its proximity to Greece and Rome, from which we obtained the first records of civilization in the Mediterranean world, but African culture extended far up the Nile into Ethiopia, a highly civilized Negro land, where it experienced a development at times superior to the culture of Egypt. When Egypt was too weak to resist the invading hordes from Asia, Ethiopia had a government sufficiently developed to repel these attacks. In the course of time Egypt became subject to the domination of Ethiopian kings who ruled it as a dependency.

During these years the world was generally ignorant of the rise and fall of African empires in the interior, for the reason that the great desert separated these people of northern Africa from the other part of the continent save to the extent that communication could be effected through the Egyptian and Ethiopian empires. No actual history of the other parts of Africa seems to have come to light until the invasion by the Mohammedans about the year 1000. It is known, however, that the Zulu kings whose armies swept southern Africa exhibited unusual power of military organization. Local chiefs, through their diplomacy, bravery, and wisdom, molded the scattered tribes of wide areas into successful kingdoms maintained by strong central governments. In the Sudan the Negroes, even prior to the coming of the Mohammedans, organized kingdoms and empires which flourished for centuries. Within these limits sprang up flourishing towns holding annual fairs attended by thousands of people from afar. These cities, moreover, were beautifully bedecked by public buildings showing a distinct advancement in architecture, as is evidenced by relics discovered when the country was explored in 1850. In these centers of Africa there developed a provincial system, judicial procedures, and the custom of prosecution and defense.

The art too of these Africans was not to be despised. The museums of leading European cities show remarkable designs in the scepters of African kings carved in hard wood, in the beautiful basketry, the symmetrical lance heads, axes inlaid in copper and decorated with filigree. There are too the megaliths of Gambia, and the bronze castings of Benin which in technique have excelled anything in European art. In fact the relics of this civilization indicate the thrift and ingenuity and the application to occupations that required not only industry, but also mechanical skills and inventive genius.

After the Mohammedan invasion the historian is able to pick up sufficient fragments to convince him of further achievements. The Mohammedans coming into this country as traders and engaging in the slave trade carried to their homes and harems in Asia and especially in Arabia certain Negroes, who by their dint of energy and unusual mental power, thoroughly demonstrated that they were persons of a superior order. A striking example of this is Antar, a slave taken into Arabia where he arose rapidly as one of the greatest poets and by his exploits in war became the hero of the land. These blacks in Arabia constituted what is called Arabised Negroes.

Empire building received a new impetus on the coming of the Mohammedans. Among these new states were the kingdom of Ghana, which experienced its golden age in the eleventh century, and the kingdom of Melle, at its best in the thirteenth century. There was an advanced civilization in the city-state of Jenne from which the modern name Guinea is derived. Around this city developed a group of smaller states which exhibited a high political organization and advanced culture. Their achievements in clay, stone, iron, glass and earthenware, weaving and art, favorably impressed Frobenius. This city experienced, as usual, migrations frequent in other parts of Africa, destroying many of the evidences of civilization. There were other such groups around Timbuctoo and Hausa where government had reached the state of that of the autonomy of modern times resembling the social or industrial state of a democratic order. These achievements so impressed the world that in keeping with other claims based on prejudice, white men have undertaken to accredit whites with this culture.

In the mining district of the lake region of Africa appeared other evidence of advancement. There the Africans were the first to smelt iron and to use it as the great leverage of civilization by which the world has been enabled to accomplish its wonders in modern times. When the Greeks, the Romans, and the Mesopotamians were still in the stone age, these progressive people had learned to make implements

of iron to solve the problem of easily earning a subsistence and to control the forces of nature. They had,
therefore, well-constructed buildings and fortifications
and as indicated by their utensils and implements,
they had made much more advancement than many
other peoples of the mediaeval times and had constructed temples comparing favorably with those of
other ancients. Among such less advanced peoples as
the Ashanti and Dahomey, who practiced the orgies
of war and the sacrifice of human beings, there was
no such progress in industry, religion, or art.

The greatest of all of these empires was the Song-
hai. This empire, according to well-authenticated records, was founded about the year 700 and continued
to about 1335 with three well-connected dynasties distinguished by great warriors who extended the territory of the empire and by statesmen who distinguished
themselves in administering its affairs. It fell prey to
the Mohammedans who about the year 1000 invaded
the continent, but by accepting the faith of that land
its greatness was not easily diminished. It boasted of
its greatest ruler in the person of Soni Ali, noted for
his military exploits and his success as a statesman.
The country again saw something like a return to a
golden age under another distinguished ruler. Under
Mohammed Askia this country extended its territory
over the small kingdoms, and brought it into contact

with Egypt and the outer world. He then organized a government on the order of the Roman provincial system and ruled as an emperor. He, moreover, promoted education in providing for the study of law, literature, and the natural sciences and medicine. Some of the achievements in modern surgery which now excite the administration of the world were common in these parts of Africa during the golden age of this empire.

It was unfortunate too that when Africa was disturbed by the continuous Mohammedan invasion promoted by the slave trade, destructive forces within contributed to its decline. The tribes of the south and the interior became restless, and in their onward march in quest of more desirable prey they swept over these centers of civilization which could not withstand the attack. A large number of wars immediately ensued and the scepter of the empire shifted from hand to hand until Africa, in its state of prostration, became the victim of a second blow at its civilization in the person of the Christian slave trader developed by commercial expansion, which was then the dominant thought of modern Europe. They encouraged the intertribal wars at the expense of Africa merely to supply the colonies of the western world with cheap slave labor, the essential factor required in the exploitation of the resources in this new land of treasures. While then the nations of Europe were emerging from the chaos of the Middle Ages, the people of Africa were being separated, divided, and scattered at their expense to serve as a tool for the adventurers in America.

This destruction of a promising civilization, however, did not mean the mental deterioration of the people of Africa. Africans who were from time to time given an opportunity for mental development in foreign lands showed that no such decline could be charged to the account of the black race. Among these were Miguel Kapranzine, J. E. J. Captein, A. W. Amo, Francis Williams, and Adjai Crowther. Kapranzine was an African taken by the Portuguese in Africa in 1631 and sent to Goa as a prisoner, but finally turned over to the Dominicans to be educated at the expense of the government. His education was directed largely toward the clerical order, and some years thereafter he became one of the greatest preachers in Portuguese India. As an appreciation of his service and worth to the church, the order conferred upon him the degree of Master of Theology in 1670 and exalted him to the position of vicar of the convent of Santa Barbara in Goa.[2]

J. E. J. Captein was brought from the jungles of west Africa by slave traders in 1742 and was educated at the University of Lyden, where he distinguished himself in Latin, Greek, Hebrew, and Chaldean and obtained his degree in theology, writing a thesis in Latin, which, strange to say, was a defense of slavery as an institution consistent with Christian liberty. He afterwards served as a missionary to Elmina in Guinea.

A. W. Amo, a native of west Africa, was brought to Amsterdam in 1707 where he was given an opportunity to be educated under the direction of his benefactor, the Duke of Brunswick. He attended the University of Halle and Wittenburg. At Halle he took the degree of Doctor of Philosophy with a dissertation entitled "De Jure Maurorum." He then qualified as a University lecturer or professor and offered regular courses at Wittenberg in 1734. He was well grounded in Dutch, German, Latin, Greek, and Hebrew and wrote several philosophical treaties in Latin. In recognition of his attainments and professional services the Prussian government conferred upon him the honor of Geheim-Ral. After thirty years' residence in Europe as a scholar and gentleman he returned to Africa to render his people distinguished service.

Another example of the enlightened Negro of this class appeared in the West Indies. This was Francis Williams, the son of one John Williams, an African slave liberated because of meritorious service and in 1708 ranked among those persons on the island against whom slave testimony was forbidden. These same privileges were extended to other members of

this family, which attached to them unusual importance among the white people with whom they moved
socially. We have much more information about his
son Francis. The family was of such good report and
the youth Francis had exhibited so many evidences of
mental capacity that early in the eighteenth century
the Duke of Montague, desiring to put to test some
of his opinions about the capabilities of the Negro,
had Francis instructed in an elementary school in Jamaica and then sent to an English grammar school to
prepare for Cambridge University. After some years
Francis Williams completed his education at Cambridge University and returned to Jamaica between
1738 and 1748.

Impressed more than ever with the truth that a
Negro trained in the same way as a white man will
have the same intellectual attainments, the Duke of
Montague sought further to advance his protégé by
securing for him a seat in the Jamaica Council. This
proposition, however, was opposed by Governor Tre-
lawny, who contended that admitting a black man
to the Council would excite restlessness among the
slaves. Whether or not the governor was diplomatic
or prejudiced is not known. He did add a Negro attachment to the army employed in Jamaica, but the
ambitious youth never sat in the Council. He settled
in Spanish Town, the capital of the island, and dur-

ing the rest of his life conducted a classical school. In this position he made a reputation for himself as a schoolmaster and figured somewhat prominently as a poet. The only evidence of his attainments in this field, however, consists of a Latin poem which conforms in most respects to the requirements of that age. It seemed, however, that he was not very popular among his own people, as he was regarded as haughty and opinionated, treating his fellow blacks with contempt and entertaining a rather high opinion of his own knowledge. He was also charged with being a deliberate sycophant and racial toady who said and did much to do his race harm.

Occasionally too the slave traders brought from Africa men who had already experienced unusual mental development. Such was the case of Michael Denton, a slave sold in the colony of Maryland. In his daily application of things religious and educational, he began to attract attention, but like the barbarians who enslaved the philosopher of Athens, his white master did not think for a moment that these exhibitions of peculiar interest in the seemingly mystified world were evidences of mental and moral development. For example, when Denton one day knelt, bowing toward Mecca to offer prayer, the son of his master threw sand in his eyes and stoned him. In the course of time, however, there appeared a man who knew a little Arabic. He easily discovered that Denton was well versed in this language and that prior to his enslavement he had attained a position of distinction among his fellows in Africa. Hearing this, James Oglethorpe interceded and effected Denton's release from slavery. He was then taken to England and introduced to a professor of Oriental languages at Cambridge, where when tested, Denton proved to be a profound scholar. This professor employed him as an assistant in the translation of Eastern manuscripts and introduced him to people of distinction, among whom he passed as a man of superior worth.

In 1812 appeared another distinguished character in the person of Adjai Crowther, born at Uchugo in the Yoruba country in west Africa. Captured there by slave traders and passing from hand to hand until he was eighteen years of age, he fell among the missionary authorities in Sierra Leone, where he was given instruction in the fundamentals, in which he made such rapid progress that he was of service in the first Niger expedition in 1841. He was then sent to England, and after studying a year at the Church Missionary Society's college at Islington, was ordained a clergyman of the Anglican church. To make himself useful to his own people he returned to Africa. He took part in the expeditions of 1854 and 1857, which enabled him to contribute much to the study of African geography and philology. He returned to England in 1864 when he was made Bishop of the Niger territory. He soon came back to Africa and served his people until 1891, the time of his death. He had then distinguished himself as a geographer and as a philologist, rendering a public service recognized by the Royal Geographic Society of London, which voted him a gold watch. He also made linguistic maps of the Niger region, valuable thereafter in the study of the modern languages of Africa, wrote several religious works and school books, and translated the Bible into the Yoruba language. In recognition of his attainments as a scholar, the University of Oxford conferred upon him the degree of Doctor of Divinity.

Notes

1 A. B. Ellis, *The Yoruba-Speaking Peoples of the Slave Coast of West Africa Their Religion, Manners, Customs, Laws, Language Etc: With an Appendix Containing a Comparison of The Etshi, Ga, Ewe and Yoruba Languages* (London: Chapman & Hall, Ltd, 1894) and Ellis, *The Tshi-Speaking Peoples of the West Coast of Africa* (Chicago: Benin Press, 1964. Repr. of 1887 ed.). Felix Dubois, *Timbuctoo: The Mysterious* (London: Hinemann, 1897).

2 Alexander Francis Chamberlain, "The Contribution of the Negro to Human Civilization," in *Select Discussions of Race Problems,* edited by J. A. Bingham, *The Atlanta University Publications, No. 20* (Atlanta: The Atlanta University Press, 1916), pp. 94-97.

3

Achievements in Captivity

Even among the whites, who as a master class wrung their bread from the sweat of the bondmen's brow, the Negroes have proved that under adverse circumstances they can do what their so-called superiors do. The privilege thus to make a record for themselves, however, was obtained only after a long period and with difficulty. It was thought that there should be no objection to the enslavement of the Negroes since they were not Christians and, according to an unwritten law, persons who did not believe in Christianity could be enslaved. When, however, in response to a general objection to slavery, masters had to make the argument that the institution would be a blessing to the Negroes in that it would enable them to adopt Christianity and western civilization, they faced the alternative of either bringing the Negroes from Africa merely to have them converted and freed or of abrogating this unwritten law so far as it concerned Negroes.

By certain proclamations of the Bishop of London and the formal statutes of the colonies it was soon decided that this principle did not apply to the blacks.

In the course of time, however, the life of the Negroes in the new world, although that of hewers of wood or drawers of water, was not necessarily a hopeless one. Many masters felt that to increase the economic efficiency of their slaves they should be given all of the enlightenment possible. Negroes were, therefore, instructed in the home, in the parish schools, and in certain private institutions, that they might absorb western civilization as rapidly as possible and thus equip themselves to function more efficiently in the exploitation of the New World.

Another door of hope was open to Negroes in the possibility of effecting their manumission by purchase or meritorious service. This custom among the French and Spanish gave rise to a large number of freedmen. In certain colonies of the West Indies, these multiplied to the extent that sufficient encouragement was afforded the slaves to abandon their masters and live in the remote districts and in the mountains, where they constituted a class known as Maroons. In parts where the Negroes were as numerous as the whites, these fugitives often jeopardized the very life of the colony. They had few arms that the primitive man did not possess, but because of their resourcefulness and power in military organization they became a source of much terror throughout Latin America. In the small colony of Guatemala in the seventeenth century, there were as many as three hundred such Negroes who had resorted to the woods and could not be subdued by the forces sent against them.

The greatest enterprise of the Maroon, how-ever, was exhibited not by any particular individual but rather by that of the little Negro Republic in Brazil, called Palmares, styled by Professor Charles E. Chapman as the Negro Numantia, because its career resembles so much of Numantia against which the Romans fought for a number of years before they could invade the beleaguered city. Because of the bad treatment of the Portuguese slaves, many of those imported from Guinea escaped to the forests, where they established villages called quilombos, the type to which Palmares, in the Province of Pernambuco, belonged. It was not long, however, before this town extended its sway over a number of other settled persons of the same antecedents. At one time it was reported to have a population of twenty thousand, with ten thousand fighting men. Palmares, the name also of the capital of the republic, was surrounded by wooden walls made of trunks of trees and entered by huge gates provided with facilities for wide surveillance and sentry service.

Over time the population of this village gradually increased because of the eagerness of slaves and freemen to try their fortunes in the forests. In the beginning, they maintained themselves by a sort of banditry, taking food, slaves, and women, whether mulatto, black, or white. They later settled down to agriculture, and established seemingly peaceful trade relations with the Portuguese settlements in the less hostile parts of Brazil. Palmares then developed into a sort of nation, uniting the desirable features of the republican and monarchial forms of government, presided over by a chief executive called the Zombe, who ruled with absolute power during life. "The right to candidacy," says Professor Chapman, "was restricted to a group recognized as composing the bravest men in the community. Any man in the state might aspire to this dignity providing he had Negro blood in his veins."

In the English colonies during the eighteenth century this group never became more than a thrifty class of free Negroes. Some of these, however, became persons of unusual worth and even of distinction. Among those in the literary world may be mentioned Jupiter Hammon, a writer of religious verse exhibiting an appreciation of his position as a slave and his dependence on God. There appeared later Phillis Wheatley, a more enlightened and a much better known person of literary bearing, who by her writings impressed the general public of her day and brought herself into friendly relations with some of the most distinguished people of the time. Of this same order was another free Negro, known by the nom de plume of "Othello," a writer of a number of valuable essays on the intolerable condition of the Negroes in captivity among the whites. In these productions he exhibited evidence of the advantages of a liberal education. No man could today set forth the claims of the Negro in a more eloquent and convincing style than did "Othello" in 1788. More famous than all other Negroes of his time, however, was Benjamin Banneker, the mathematician and astronomer. He invented the first clock made in the United States and published one of the first series of almanacs produced in this country. Few white men had then achieved so much in these useful fields.

There were too among the Negroes intelligent and forceful preachers like George Liele, the founder of the first Negro Baptist Church of Savannah, Georgia, and the organizer of the first Baptist Church in Kingston, Jamaica. Andrew Bryan, Liele's successor in Savannah, a man of some education, and the owner of property including slaves, was an attractive figure in Georgia from 1790 to 1815. John Jacob was an unusual preacher of such good standing among all classes that he was chosen the pastor of a white Baptist Church in Portsmouth, Virginia. Harry Hosier and "Black Harry" preached with success to groups of both races. More distinguished than all of these was Lemuel Haynes of Burlington, Vermont, the son of a white woman and a Negro slave. In spite of his color he attained distinction as a preacher to the whites in his section, serving successfully three New England congregations.

These opportunities for the Negro to rise above the status of slavery were multiplied during the American Revolution when manumission was facilitated by favorable laws enacted during this period and when most of the states of the North (where few slaves were found) provided for gradual emancipation. After the ardor for natural rights had passed away there came the industrial revolution effected by various inventions culminating with the cotton gin, revolutionizing the industrial world, which exhibited an apparent need for the slave plantation to supply the world with cotton fiber. Thereafter the aim was to reduce the Negroes to the plane of the primitive people. It was at this time that we find recorded in the literature and official documents throughout the United States a protest against any encouragement of the Negro to be other than that of a beast of burden and the rise of that literature which has had for its purpose to scandalize and to humiliate the race by the propagation of untruths as to its inherent inferiority.

It is from such writers that the people of our own day take their information and from such documents as our so-called scholars obtain most of their evidence as to what the Negro has thought and felt and done. Some of these slanderers have to a very great extent succeeded in convincing the world of the justice of enslaving and oppressing the Negroes because of a divine plan to assign each race a special role in the drama of history in accordance with its peculiar mental endowments. The study of the eighteenth-century Negroes in the United States, the ones who exhibited all tendencies of the ability of the Negro to rise in the midst of an environment offering better opportunities, has therefore been neglected. These biased writers hold up before the world not what the Negro has done, but what he has not done during the years that his oppressor has had the privilege of driving him as a beast and even murdering him when he could no longer endure, as the Belgians recently did in the Congo.

During the years when the Negroes had a chance for advancement, theirs differed very little from that of the white man. There was among them a class of free Negroes who because of the education and the general culture which they had experienced ranked not only above the slaves but far above many of the whites. In fact, a large number of these free Negroes were descendants of masters and had such little Negro blood in them that they easily passed over to the other race, for in those days the status of men was determined not so much by their race as by what they stood for in the community. As a matter of fact, the court records prior to the Civil War give numerous instances of Negroes who after toiling up from poverty to positions of wealth and influence had themselves declared white by establishing the fact that they had less than one-eighth of Negro blood.

The reader of a biased mind who gives credence to the reports and misinformation found in most books concerning the Negro will unconsciously explain away these claims to unusual achievement by saying that these Negroes were exceptions standing out like shining lights in the midst of a great darkness. When one considers, however, the unusually promising economic progress which the Negroes experienced during these years, such suspicions must vanish from the mind. It is a well known truth that not only drudgery but the higher pursuits of labor were followed by the slaves and freedmen of the South prior to the Civil War. The white man's disinclination to engage in labor but to live on the labor of someone else prevented the whites as a group from developing an exclusive class of mechanics or artisans. Availing themselves of this economic opportunity, the Negroes amassed sums sufficiently large to provide themselves with the comforts of life denied them by their masters, and sometimes accumulated amounts adequate to the purchase of their freedom, which placed them during the early days of the republic on a basis of equality with most of the poor whites.

This condition of affairs obtained even in the nineteenth century. The reports of the United States census covering the period between 1790 and 1915 give some interesting facts. In Charleston, South Carolina, in 1848 there were 50 pilots and sailors, 120 carpenters, 68 masons and bricklayers, 16 painters and plasterers, 51 ship carpenters and joiners, 61 coopers, 40 blacksmiths, 36 tailors and cap makers, 39 bakers, 43 apprentices, and 45 other mechanics among the slaves. Among the free Negroes of the same city that year there were 18 confectioners, 196 seamstresses and mantua makers, 7 milliners, 6 tailors and cap makers, and 5 fruiterers. In 1850 Louisiana had 11 Negro apprentices, 26 blacksmiths, 39 boatmen, 25 teachers, 24 cabinet makers, 521 carpenters, 169 cigar makers, 56 coopers, 158 farmers, and 13 gardeners. Most of these people lived in the city of New Orleans, as the majority of Negroes thus employed were confined to urban communities. In New York City there were 21 boatmen, 28 bookbinders, 33 butchers, 39 car men, 12 carpenters, 9 doctors, 3 druggists and 24 farmers, 2 hatters, 434 mariners, 21 ministers, 24 musicians,

23 shoemakers, 23 tailors, 8 teachers, 4 lawyers, and 3 merchants. In the state of Connecticut there were 10 basket makers, 13 car men, 146 farmers, 316 mariners, 4 mechanics, 2 merchants, 12 musicians, one printer, one sail maker, 41 shoe makers, 9 tailors, and one tanner.

Out of this class grew a small but more successful group of Negroes who used their accumulations during their years of freedom to lay a foundation for a higher status than that of a mere tradesman. These became small farmers, planters, and businessmen. Negroes purchased considerable land a long time before the reaction in the South during the first quarter of the nineteenth century became effective in restricting them in this sphere. The court records of Northampton County, Virginia, show that in 1653 Anthony Johnson, a Negro slaveholder, owned 250 acres of land. Andrew Bryan, a preacher of Savannah, Georgia, during the last of the eighteenth century and the first decade of the nineteenth century was the owner of a farm outside of the city in charge of his eight slaves. A Negro minister of Lexington, Kentucky, owned $20,000 worth of property in 1830. Austin Dabney, of Walton County, a remarkable free man of color, was given a large tract of land by the legislature of Georgia because of the valuable service he rendered the country during the Revolutionary War. Upon this he established himself as a planter living above want and deserving the consideration of his white neighbors, among whom he lived on terms of equality and whose respect and confidence he enjoyed until he died. The Cromwell family, the descendants of whom are now living in Washington, District of Columbia, came into possession of a large tract of land in Virginia but were unfortunately deprived of it by shrewd whites. A number of Negro veterans of the war of 1812 and their descendants, by virtue of a decision given by the attorney general serving under Andrew Jackson, came into possession of certain bounty lands long withheld from them on the ground that they were persons of color.

Negroes were also slaveholders, accepted in some cases as socially equal to the whites themselves. The world would be surprised at a thorough digest of the large number of Negroes that actually owned scores of slaves, for so many of our day are of the impression that the status was peculiar to the whites. As a matter of fact, however, when the Negroes were freed by the success of the Union cause, a number of Negro slaveholders regretted it as much as whites did. John H. Russell has all but proved that one of the first Negroes brought to our shores in 1619 became a slaveholder.[1] A bill of sale in the possession of the Connecticut Historical Society at Hartford shows that in 1783 one Prince, a free Negro, sold a slave woman to Isaac Dennison. The deed books of St. Augustine, Florida, have a record of the sale of a Negro worth $300 to Joseph Sanchez, a colored carpenter, in 1785. In 1795 Juan Batista Lusser and Julia Vilard and Simon Andrey were reported as Negro slaveholders. That same year George Radford, a free Negro of Henrico County, Virginia, was returned also as a slaveholder. Not far from Newbern there lived one John Carruthers Stanley, in Craven County, North Carolina, where he acquired considerable property. He was the owner of 64 slaves and at the same time had bound to him by law of service 42 other Negroes. He then owned two large plantations near Newbern where he owned town property. On account of unfortunate speculations in unwise investments he lost practically all of his wealth before his death. In the same city of Newbern lived Duncan Montford, a dark mulatto, who also owned slaves, among whom was Isaac Rue, a mason by trade, a grandson of whom became in later years the postmaster of the city of Newbern.

A Negro named Nathaniel Butler living near Aberdeen, Harford County, Maryland, was not only a slaveholder but a slave trader. He exercised his shrewdness by persuading bondsmen to escape from their masters to a place which he beforehand had prepared. He would then seek the master and find out how much he would take for the runaway slaves. As the price of course would be determined largely by the hope of recapturing the fugitive, Butler could easily buy the slave at a greatly reduced price. His place, therefore, became one of refuge for fugitives but upon being exposed he lost the confidence not only of white people but of Negroes as well, and efforts were made to take his life. A Negro named Dabouca, who lived until 1906 near Mobile, was during the days of slavery the owner of several bondmen. John Pous, son of a white father and a Negro mother, owned many slaves in Pensacola, Florida. He went with his slaves into the Civil War and fought with them on the side of the Union Army.

A faithful Negro belonging to Thomas Blackwell in Vance County, North Carolina, was allowed to purchase his own freedom and he afterwards became the owner of several slaves himself. Among other slaveholders in that section were William Chavers, a well-educated Negro and owner of much land, and John Sampson, a man of consequence in Wilmington. During the thirties Judith Angus of Petersburg and Mary Quickley and Reuben West of Richmond were well-known slaveholders. Among the Negro slaveholders of Maryland was Elenor Linkin, who had three persons and two slaves in her home. Alethia Tanner of Alexandria, Virginia, purchased her freedom in 1818 for $1,400 and later that of her sister Lorina Cook and five children in 1826. Out of this group developed the famous Cook family, which has rendered valuable service in the District of Columbia. It is remarkable too that when the Negroes of the District of Columbia were emancipated by a compensation process in 1862, one Negro received $2,168 for 10 slaves, another $832 for 2, a third $43.80 for one, and a fourth $547.50 for one, while from the $4,073 placed to the credit of the Sisters of the Visitation of Georgetown, $298.75 was deducted by Ignacious Tillman toward the purchase of the freedom of his family.

In the fifties when Mr. F. Law Olmsted was making his journeys throughout the South, he found in Louisiana three plantations that were owned by colored men who bought black folks and had servants of their own. In going down the Cane River, Olmsted found a number of free colored planters. He was informed by the captain of the vessel that in fifteen miles of a well-situated and cultivated country on the bank of the river beginning ten miles below Natchitoches, he did not know but one pure-blooded white man. The plantations, he said, appeared in no way different from those of the white Creoles and on some of them were large, handsome, and comfortable houses. The free colored people were descendants from the progeny of the old French and Spanish planters and their Negro slaves. Olmsted was informed also by a white man, whom he met in Washington after he had traveled through the state of Louisiana, that free Negroes of the state in general, so far as he had observed, were equal in all respects to the whites. The best houses and most tasteful grounds that he had visited in the state, he said, "belonged to a nearly full blooded Negro—a very dark man." He and his family were well educated, and though French was their native tongue, they spoke English with freedom, and one of them with much more eloquence than most liberally educated whites in the South. Cyprian Ricaud, a free man belonging to this group, caused much comment when he bought the famous Harrison property of more than 1,600 acres and 100 Negroes in the rear of Madame C. Ricaud's plantation. The Ricauds then owned 4,000 acres and 250 slaves, making this family probably the richest one of color in the world. Most Negroes of this class have since passed into the other race as whites.

Many of these Negro slaveholders, however, were not interested in the institution as such but used it as a means of philanthropic effort on behalf of their own people. There lived in Louisville, Kentucky, a colored woman named Fannie Cannady who owned her husband, a drunken cobbler whom she was able to reform somewhat by threatening to sell him down the river, if he did not mend his steps. One Jacob, a Negro, became the slave of Judge William Gaskin of Newbern, North Carolina. He then married a free woman who had a free-born son, according to law.

When the son grew up he purchased his father, but in the course of time when the elderly gentleman undertook to reprove the son for an offence committed, the young man sold his father to a slave trader who sent him far south. A free Negro living in Charleston, South Carolina, purchased for a wife a slave woman. Some years thereafter, when she ceased to behave herself as he felt that she should, he sold her for $750.00 realizing $50 on the bargain. John Nowell of Cumberland County, Virginia, sold his purchased wife to secure the necessary fee to pay an attorney to clear him of the charge that he had turned his manumission papers over to his wife's slave sweetheart, to whom she had given these documents to facilitate their elopement. In the city of Columbus, Georgia, lived a free woman of color called Disley Pope, who owned her husband. Because he offended her in some way, she, in the midst of a mental flareback, sold him to a planter, an act for which she repented thereafter and which she tried to remedy by purchasing him from his buyer, but the owner refused to accede to her request.

Some of these cases were pathetic. A free Negro carpenter named Charlie Cobb of Montgomery, Alabama, owned a Negro named George whom he maintained with some difficulty that he might not suffer the hardships of the drudgery of slavery, although he could have obtained a rather high price for him in the market. Rose Petepher of Newbern, North Carolina, married a slave named Richard Gaskin whom she afterward purchased. A woman of color in Charleston, South Carolina, obtained her husband in the same manner. James Scott, a colored man of some note residing in Harford County, Maryland, bought himself a wife and children by hiring all of them for ten years to pay off the indebtedness. Another Negro in that region was said to have sold his children in order to purchase his wife and set her free. Philip Cooper of Gloucester County, Virginia, was owned by his free wife. Peter Hakins of Richmond, Betsey Fuller of Norfolk, and Daniel Webster of Prince William County acquired titles to slaves to better their condition. Richard Hunter of Laurens County, undertook to purchase himself, but his master having died before the affair was consummated, the sum was forfeited. He was later purchased on the installment plan by his wife, a free woman, who paid several hundred dollars for him. A Negro in North Carolina, a blacksmith by trade, married a slave woman by whom he had several children. He raised sufficient money to purchase them, but held them as slaves, as there was at that time a strong sentiment against manumission.

Learning from the white man too, the Negroes shared with them the undesirable distinction of being the purchasers and masters of transported white people who were brought into this country and indentured as servants. J. H. Russell, in his treatment of colored freemen owning slaves in Virginia, believes that there was a possibility of the Negroes carrying their acquisition of this sort of property to this extent and that on this account it was necessary for the General Assembly to enact that "No negro or Indian though baptized and enjoyed their own freedoms shall be capable of any purchase of Christians but yet not debarred from buying any of their owne nation." Mr. Calvin D. Wilson, who has made an extensive study in this field, reports a purchase by free Negroes of two families of Germans who had not been able to pay their passage from Amsterdam to Baltimore and were sold for their passage money to a term of labor according to a volume issued in 1818 in Stuttgart. "It contains letters written in 1817," he says, "addressed from Baltimore to the Baron von Gagern, a minister plenipotentiary to the Diet in Frankfort on the Main. The Germans of Baltimore were so outraged by this action that they immediately got together a purse and bought the freedom of these immigrants."[2] Having the same fear which actuated the enactment of a prohibition of such acquisitions of property, most of the slaveholding states followed the example of Virginia.

To what extent then did the Negro figure as a slaveholder? No accurate information can be obtained, but the United States census reports throw much light on this question. In 1790 there were 48 Negro slave-holders owning 143 slaves in Maryland when there were 8,043 free Negroes in the state. In 1835, 213 free Negroes in the city of New Orleans owned 640 slaves when there were about 426 such slaveholders in the whole state of Louisiana. In 1860 there were in Charleston 132 Negroes paying taxes on slaves and there were 264 such Negroes in the whole state of South Carolina. This meant that one out of every 38 Negroes owned slaves. On this basis it has been esti-mated that more than 18,000 slaves were owned by Negroes during the period of slavery. If then the insti-tution of slavery had existed longer and the Negroes themselves by a special effort resulting in special laws to this effect had not been barred from that class of property holders, this number would have been con-siderably larger and the tendency on the part of the Negro to rank himself economically as the equal of the white man would have been manifested to much greater effect.

The Negroes who succeeded in escaping from their captivity in the South to enjoy more free-dom in the North exhibited further evidences of their ability to accumulate wealth and vie with the white man in the economic world. Most of these Negroes purchased their freedom, whereas some others escaped their masters to the settlements where they established homes, schools, churches, and benevolent societies. Where the trade unions did not proscribe them, many of them entered the higher pursuits of labor and accumulated funds with which they entered business. Among these may be mentioned such captains of industry as Henry Boyd, a manufacturer; Robert Gordon, a coal dealer; and Samuel F. Wilcox, a wholesale grocer worth $60,000, all of Cincinnati, Ohio; Lomax B. Cook, a broker; and Richard De Baptist, a contractor, both of Detroit; James Forten, a sail manufacturer; Joseph Casey, a broker; Stephen Smith, a lumber merchant; and William H. Riley, a boot maker, all of Philadelphia; Stephen Mulber, a contractor of Steubenville, Ohio; and David Jenkins, a household decorator of Columbus.

Other figures indicate too that this progress was not confined to a few persons. In 1847 the Negroes of Philadelphia owned $400,000 worth of property. The free blacks of Cincinnati were worth $209,000 in 1840, and in Baltimore they had sufficient property to afford a school tax of $500. In the remote districts too this same spirit of progress among Negroes was exhibited. In Mercer County, Ohio, the Negroes took up 20,000 acres of land. In southern Indiana they owned as many as 30,000 acres. Negro landowners in various other settlements among the Quakers and congenial whites in the North were considered common, as in the case of the settlement of Negroes in Cass County, Michigan.

Notes

1   John H. Russell, "Colored Freemen as Slave Owners in Virginia," *The Journal of Negro History*, Vol. 1, No. 3 (Jun., 1916), pp. 233-242.

2   Calvin D. Wilson, "Black Masters," in *North American Review*, CLXXXI, 685-698, and "Negroes Who Owned Slaves," in *Popular Science Monthly*, LXXXI, 483-494.

4

Achievements in Spite of Handicap

One of the important tests of the advance of a race is whether or not it has solved the problem of earning a subsistence. The Negroes were finally freed in this country, but many doubted that they would be able to take care of themselves. In this respect, however, the Negroes have measured up to a standard of high efficiency. The sphere of the race has been labor and drudgery, but accepting the situation without complaint, they have cheerfully worked in their restricted sphere for the necessities and comforts of life.

Some effort has been made to charge the Negro with shiftlessness and to account for the same by referring to the situation in Africa, out of which the ancestors of the ex-slaves came. An advanced civilization has not been expected in a tropical climate in which there is no struggle for life, except far from the equator in the agricultural and cattle zones, where earning a subsistence is more problematic and consequently more efficiency is required to provide against suffering from the pain of hunger. This idea as to the influence of the former life of the Negro in Africa on his economic life in this country, however, is too far-fetched to claim the attention of scientists. The fact is that the Negroes were brought into this country and broken in to toil in the worst sort of drudgery, which was their lot for two and one-half centuries. It cannot be believed, therefore, that industrial training under such adverse circumstances and hardships during so long a period would have no effect in the transformation of the Negro as a laboring class. This more recent comment, however, comes largely from the unhistorical attitude of writers of biased accounts covering the Reconstruction period, when thousands of Negroes suddenly emancipated wandered as vagrants from the country into towns and cities, believing in that way they could best enjoy their freedom. These writers in urging such conclusions disregard the fact that while there were thousands of vagrants during the first few months after the Negroes were emancipated, there were millions who were at work and remained so without interruption.

The great trouble with these accusers is that *they* rather than the Negroes need to learn to work. If the Negroes did not learn to work when imported into the

United States because of character developed in Africa, they have, nevertheless, learned to work so much better than their neighbors who boast of inheriting the civilization of the temperate zone. Evidently the Negroes, under a serious handicap, can do things that many white men have never learned to do. The census of 1890 showed that although the Negroes constitute 29.8% of the population of the South, about half of its agricultural laborers are Negroes. Comparing the whites with the Negroes, the census reports show that in the main the Negroes are gainfully employed, and if one would deduct from the number of whites thus listed, those engaged as peddlers, agents, and imposters, robbing Negroes under the guise of businessmen, the number to the credit of the whites would be considerably less. The trouble with so many white men today is that there are too many to live on the labor of a small number of Negroes, and there is little wonder that we hear the periodical complaints about the shiftlessness of the blacks and the necessity for teaching them to work.

In this respect there has arisen a very grave misconception with reference to the education of the Negro. So many men employing Negroes are of the opinion that the so-called industrial education of the Negro will help the employer to solve some of his present-day perplexing problems. Industrial schools have, therefore, received the endorsement of this class. The truth is, however, Hampton, Tuskegee, and the like have not had and will not have any particular bearing on teaching Negroes to work. It is sheer nonsense to think that all the Negroes of the country can be reached or materially influenced by a few schools. The Negroes knew how to work long before the founders of these institutions were born and were so engaged when they were established. The mission of the industrial school is not to lead Negroes to form habits of industry, but to emphasize the importance of skilled labor and increase the number of Negroes participating in it. It will in the end be of much assistance in the economic advancement of the Negro toward self-assertion in the industrial world, and will therefore multiply rather than solve the problems of the white employer who does not believe in proper division of the returns of labor.

Unfortunately most of these complaints as to the shiftlessness of the Negro come from white persons who have known the Negroes only through the servants attached to their homes. Negroes of this class are no longer representative of that better class of servants who worked in the homes of their masters prior to the Civil War. These former servants are no more and their descendants have in freedom elevated themselves above this status. They are now physicians, preachers, and teachers to their people. A considerable number of them have purchased farms and established businesses of their own. Those left far down to constitute the class of menial servants of the white man are too often the riff-raff of the Negro race, many of whom are afflicted with filth, vice, and disease. Yet, because of the upward strides of those Negroes who are moving in a different sphere, the white people in certain sections are reluctant to concede them a higher standard of efficiency and of moral and social worth than that evidenced by the undesirables attached to them as servants.

The whole question, moreover, comes back to this fundamental thing: If these Negro servants are so unsatisfactory, why is it that it is necessary for whites still to employ Negroes? Cannot their own men and women work? Are they so lacking in civilization as not yet to have solved the problem of dignifying labor? It cannot be argued that all white men are rich. The point is as already stated that too many white men have not as yet learned the lesson that they desire to teach the Negroes, namely, that work is honorable, while at the same time they unconsciously teach the white youth that it is dishonorable. The reports of the United States Census show that in proportion to population the laboring class of the South is black rather than white. If then we concede that the Negroes are shiftless and cannot be induced to work, how do we account for the various industries in operation in that country and for the farms which have recently shown marked steps forward in agricultural progress? Who is doing this labor?

The census reports will help us further to determine what the Negroes in this country have been doing. 5,192,535 or 71% of the 7,317,922 Negroes aged ten years and over were reported in 1910 as gainfully employed. 2,893,375 were engaged in agriculture, forestry, and animal husbandry. 2,125,387 or 29% of this group were not gainfully employed. In the number employed in agriculture are included 893,370 farmers, planters, and overseers operating farms of 42,279,310 acres with property thereon worth $1,141,792,526. Of the number operating farms, 218,972 were owners, 672,964 tenants, and 1,434 managers, of 24.5%, 75.3%, and 2% respectively. Owners free of debt possessed 8,835,857 acres, owners having mortgaged farms had 4,011,491 acres, and part owners 2,844,188 acres. There were 12,876,308 acres operated by cash tenants, 13,691,494 by share tenants, and 349,779 by managers. This area of 42,279,510 acres will appear more realistic when one considers that it is as large as New England or Belgium and Holland combined.

Negroes do not despise agriculture, but a considerable number of them have gone into other fields to exhibit evidence of the value of the race for skilled labor. In 1910, for example, it was reported that of 40,584 Negroes laboring in mines 182 were engineers; 157 machinists; 121 blacksmiths; 116 bosses, foremen, or overseers; and 107 cutlers. In 1910, 657,130 Negroes were engaged in manufacturing, including the hand trades. This designation embraces every occupation of this sort imaginable, and Negroes were represented in all of them. The Negro population throughout the country showed in 1910 that there were 30,464 carpenters, 12,401 brick and stone masons, 9,727 blacksmiths, 8,035 painters, 6,077 clerks, 2,318 clerks in stores, 4,802 engineers, 2,308 coopers, 4,652 tailors, 3,695 shoemakers, 3,394 salesmen in stores, 3,296 machinists, 3,232 builders and contractors, 2,756 mail carriers, and 2,285 plumbers and gas and stem fitters.

The Negroes have made achievements in other fields. Many have left the farms for the city, not to crowd denizens of vice but to engage in business. In all southern cities and in northern cities like New York, Philadelphia, Pittsburgh, and Chicago, the Negroes are gradually purchasing homes once rented and are taking over the business formerly monopolized by the whites. There is now hardly an urban Negro community of any consequence which has not a successful real estate firm, a progressive contractor, a branch of a Negro insurance company, a bank, or some other financial organization.

American Negroes have from time immemorial figured individually in the business world, but they are now learning to pool their interests for larger enterprises. The Negro fraternal organizations, although established for social purposes, have in recent years taken on a business aspect in providing for the purchase of property and the insurance of the lives of their members. In some parts of the South the Negroes use no other insurance and the managers of this work constitute in reality an industrial insurance company. The Negroes have about 50 banks and ten insurance companies, one of which is a regular old line life insurance company. 3,208 Negroes were in 1910 employed in banking and brokerage, 2,604 in insurance, and 1,095 in real estate. Among these captains of industry should be mentioned John W. Lewis, President of the Industrial Savings Bank and the Whitelaw Apartment House Corporation of Washington; Samuel W. Rutherford, Secretary of the National Benefit Association of the same city; Isaiah T. Montgomery, the founder of Mound Bayou, Mississippi; John Merrick, founder of the North Carolina Mutual and Provident Association; R.L. Smith, the founder of the Farmers Improvement Society of Texas; Heman E. Perry, President of the Standard Life Insurance Company of Atlanta; and Sara Rector, who has by inheritance become unusually rich.[1] These men own property worth more than $1,000,000,000.

To promote the economic progress of the race, Negroes have been wise enough to organize several efficient agencies. The first of these to attain importance was the Nation Business League founded by Dr. Booker T. Washington. There are also the National Negro Insurance Association, the National Negro Bankers Association, the National Association of Funeral Directors, and the National Negro Retail Merchants Association. To prevent the whites from encroaching upon the rights of Negro labor, the blacks have recently organized a national labor organization to secure to their people certain protections and privileges which they have not been able to secure even when admitted to unions represented in the American Federation of Labor.

In the professions the Negroes have done remarkably well. In proportion to the population, there are more preachers among Negroes than among the whites, whereas in the other professions the whites far exceed the blacks. This may be easily accounted for in the fact that the Negro, believing that the emotional black has a monopoly on inspiration, has responded more readily to this appeal than to that of the other Negroes qualified to render professional service. Negroes still lack confidence in lawyers of their own race, and in a few localities the physician or dentist does not find much to do if white men in these professions do not discriminate against the blacks. In 1910 there was one clergyman for every 562 Negroes and one for every 815 whites. There is a college president or professor for every 40,611 Negroes and one for every 5,301 whites; a lawyer, judge, or justice for every 12,315 Negroes and one for every 718 whites; a musician for every 1,753 Negroes and one for every 612 whites; a school teacher for every 334 Negroes and one for every 145 whites; a trained nurse for every 4,039 Negroes and one for every 1,024 whites. This, however, is a remarkable showing when one considers that the race has done practically all of this in fifty years. It is unreasonable to expect the Negroes to overtake the whites in half a century. It means no little achievement to have now 1,270 actors; 59 architects; 329 artists, sculptors, and teachers of art; 123 chemists; 237 civil and mining engineers; 478 dentists; 798 lawyers; 3,077 physicians; and 29,432 teachers.

These achievements are considered the more remarkable because of the fact that they were accomplished in spite of handicap. That the Negroes should be advancing in skilled labor is due somewhat to the fact that the disinclination of the preponderance of the white drones to work leaves open to the Negro many an inviting field. That the Negroes should enter the professions at all is a tribute to their own enterprise and to northern philanthropy, which have redeemed them from the curse of ignorance in which slavery left them, and for the extermination of which certain parts of the South have not only refused to support Negro schools with money accruing from the taxation of property of the whites but have even refused to appropriate to Negro education all of the money derived from taxing the property of Negroes for educational purposes. In some communities the Negroes, numbering almost half of the population, receive less than 15% of the school fund.

The Negro has exhibited a marked tendency toward the improvement of home conditions, which the institution of slavery prevented from developing and destroyed when developed by selling the wife from the husband, the husband from the wife, parents from children, and children from parents. Negro families increased from 1,410,769 in 1890 to 2,173,018 in 1910. Since 1890 the increase in proportion to the family development in other racial groups has varied, but in 1890 and 1900 the average size of the Negro family somewhat exceeded, and in 1910 precisely equaled, the average family of all classes combined. The Negro family exceeds the average for families in the North and West.

This development of the family exhibits further evidence of the permanence of home life in that Negroes show a general desire to own a home, to form a permanent attachment to the community. The Negroes are in no sense vagrants as some would make believe. In 1910 the Negroes of the United States owned 488,699 homes, 220,698 of which were farm homes and 268,001 other homes. Some of these homes consist of costly establishments which might pass as mansions. Among the homes of this kind may be mentioned that of Mr. Herndon in Atlanta; that of Mr. Blodgett of Jacksonville, Florida; and that of Madam C. J. Walker in New York.[2]

This exhibition of thrift is all but startling when one takes into account the adverse circumstances under which Negroes have had to accomplish this task. During these years the whites have organized a movement against the effort of Negroes to purchase desirable farmland or to get out of the squalor of the ghetto by purchasing property in the desirable parts of the cities. To keep the Negroes confined to the undesirable homes, the South has resorted to laws of segregation and mob violence, and during the recent migration of the Negroes to the North some places in that section have followed the example of the slavery-cursed South.

With the establishment of the Negro home has come a higher standard of morals. In spite of the teachings of slavery to the contrary, Negroes have well learned the importance of sexual purity. The promiscuous unions permitted in the antebellum period are now generally impossible in the face of a strong public opinion to the contrary. The incursions of lustful white men into the race have been decidedly checked by the healthy sentiment against it and the tendency of Negroes to sustain sexual relations to undesirable whites has for the same reason decreased. Experiencing a keener appreciation of woman and of the influence she wields in maintaining about her an atmosphere of chastity, the Negroes have learned to protect and defend their women, even when as in recent cases it has meant death at the hands of the mob by white brutes invading the sanctity of the Negro home.

Negroes have, moreover, with the assistance of northern philanthropists undertaken to educate themselves. In many of the school districts where the small school fund allotted the Negroes affords a term of only a few months, the patrons of the school raise money by subscription to extend the term. Adults who cannot forgo the benefits of education and have not the means to devote all of their time to the prosecution of studies establish and maintain night school to supply this special need. Negro national church organizations have been successful in founding and financing systems far superior to the schools supposed to be maintained by the state. The most effective of these agents in the promotion of the private colored schools

among the Negroes have been the African Methodist
Episcopal Church, the African Methodist Episcopal
Zion Church, the Colored Methodist Episcopal Church,
and the Baptist Church through the National Baptist
Convention.

The Negroes have access to 118 schools maintained by white independent boards and 354 supported by white denominational boards, the former with
an attendance of 14,851 and the latter 51,529. There
are also 153 schools maintained by colored churches
for the 17,299 students in attendance. In these schools
supported by Negroes there are 828 teachers, and the
property of these schools is estimated at $2,305,054.

Negro enterprise has extended beyond the point
of mere individual achievement. Largely restricted
to certain areas, the Negroes have made a few communities in various parts, essentially groups of blacks
who shape and carry out the economic, social, and
political policies of these communities. The most important of these communities are Plateau near Mobile,
Alabama; Brooklyn, Illinois; Buxton, Iowa; Mound
Bayou, Mississippi; Boley, Oklahoma; and Institute,
West Virginia. Some of the important rural communities of Negroes are Baldwin Farms and Southern
Improvement Company Settlement, Alabama; Calvin
Township, Michigan: Deo Volente, Mississippi; Snow
Hill, New Jersey; and Long, Darke County and Wil-

berforce, Greene County, Ohio.[3] They have in most cases Negro town officials, a Negro postmaster, and Negro school teacher, with white men figuring in the equation only so far as they communicate with the inhabitants of the town.

What the Negroes have accomplished in the economic world has been helpful to them in making other achievements. The fact that two Negroes sat in the United States Senate, that a score of them came to the House of Representatives, and that several of the Southern states were during the Reconstruction period ruled by Negroes and their sympathetic white friends does not now account for much credit for the Negro. That unusual and sudden exaltation of the race is now considered a calamitous anomaly in the working out of a government from the chaos resulting from the Civil War. Such an estimate, however, cannot be placed on the political recognition now being given Negroes, even in the South where in most cases a majority of the voters are white. Recently a Negro justice of the peace was elected by white voters in Alabama; seven Negroes were elected members of state legislatures in 1918, three of them in West Virginia, a former slave state; and a Negro candidate for Congress in New York received the support of some of the most substantial white people in that district.[4] A number of Negroes are annually appointed to positions of importance in state and city offices; many of the large cities employ Negro policemen; and until disturbed by a mediaeval national administration the Negroes held a fair proportion of the positions in the United States Civil Service, which they obtained by competitive examination.

Notes

1 More information on John W. Lewis, President of the Industrial Savings Bank and the Whitelaw Apartment House Corporation of Washington, DC, can be found at http://www.pbs.org/ellingtonsdc/vtOtherLandMarks.htm. For a fascinating study of Isaiah T. Montgomery and Mound Bayou, see Janet Sharp Hermann, *The Pursuit of a Dream* (Jackson: University Press of Mississippi, 1999). Samuel W. Rutherford, Secretary of the National Benefit Association of Washington, DC., was born in 1866 in Georgia, and entered business after farming. His start in insurance began with the True Reformers, and he started Beneficial in 1898 in Washington. For a biographical sketch see "Samuel W. Rutherford," *The Journal of Negro History* (April 1952), 216-217. More on R. L. Smith, the founder of the Farmers Improvement Society of Texas, can be found in Merline Pitre, *Through Many Dangers, Toils and Snares: The Black Leadership of Texas, 1868-1900* (Austin: Eakin, 1985). For a very insightful study of John Merrick and North Carolina Mutual see Walter B. Weare, *Black Business in the New South: A Social History of the North Carolina Mutual Life Insurance Company* (Durham: Duke University Press, 1993). Precious little work has been done on either Heman E. Perry or the insurance company he created, Standard Life. Similarly little remains known about Sara Rector. For more on black bankers, see Arnett G. Lindsay, "The Negro in Banking," *The Journal of Negro History*, Vol. 14, No. 2 (April 1929), 156-201.

2 On Herndon, see Carole Merritt, *The Herndons: An Atlanta Family* (Athens: University of Georgia Press, 2002). Virtually nothing has been written on Joseph H. Blodgett of Jacksonville, Florida, beyond the fact that he was believed to be a millionaire contractor. In contrast, there is much more known about Madam C. J. Walker of New York. See A'Lelia Bundles, *On Her Own Ground: The Life and Times of Madam C. J. Walker* (New York: Scribner, 2001).

3 Much of the work on black towns has focused on the West rather than the Midwest or the eastern seaboard. For a very useful bibliography of black towns in the American West, see

George H. Junne, *Blacks in the American West and Beyond—America, Canada, and Mexico: An Annotated Bibliography* (New York: Greenwoods Press, 2002). A number of first-rate studies should be consulted: Quintard Taylor, *In Search of the Racial Frontier: African Americans in the American West* (New York: W. W. Norton & Company, 1998); Norman L. Crockett, *The Black Towns* (Lawrence: The Regents Press of Kansas, 1979); and Kenneth M. Hamilton, *Black Towns and Profit* (Urbana: University of Illinois Press, 1991). On towns in the East, see Joe Mobley, "In the Shadows of White Society: Princeville, a Black Town in North Carolina, 1886-1915," *North Carolina Historical Review* (July 1986): 340-384.

4 In 1918, Rev. Reverdy Ransom ran as an Independent Republican in New York and garnered the support of Mrs. Katherine Clemmons Gould, the former wife of Howard Gould. "Negroes Hear Mrs. Gould," New York Times, February 27, 1918. Ransom was a major figure in twentieth-century America, and he is finally getting attention. See Annetta L. Gomez-Jefferson, The Sage of Tawawa: Reverdy Cassius Ransom (Kent: Kent State University Press, 2003), xi; Calvin S. Morris, Reverdy C. Ransom: Black Advocate of the Social Gospel (Lanham, Md.: University Press of America, 1990); and Anthony B. Pinn, Making the Gospel Plain: The Writings of Bishop Reverdy C. Ransom (Harrisburg: Trinity Press, 1999).

5

The Debit Side of the Ledger

As much as may be said in favor of the Negro, he, like other human beings, has faults, though not so many as the enemies of the race would make the world believe. The most striking of these and the one most generally commented on is that of the Negro's attitude toward health. A large number of people charge the race with being out of sympathy with the recent movement to direct the attitude of the world toward a larger appreciation of the laws of health and the bearing of hygiene on the development of the race. The Negroes, they say, are not personally clean. They wear soiled clothing, do not apparently bathe as often as they should, live in unclean hovels, and manifest little civic pride in keeping clean that part of the city in which they live. They, moreover, are branded as topers attached to the habit of taking strong drink and as lepers afflicted with venereal diseases.

Generally speaking, much can be said to substantiate some of these charges, but it cannot be proved that these faults are inherent in the Negro race. When adequate investigation has been made, it will appear that these conditions obtain because of the circumstances over which the Negro has little control. As to the personal cleanliness, we need but to reflect that slavery as an institution trained the Negro to be personally unclean. In spite of all precepts to the contrary, the Negro slave, unless attached to his master as a house servant, could not as such keep himself personally clean, while doomed to the lowest sort of drudgery and supplied with few of the necessities and practically no comforts of life. In freedom, moreover, the Negro has not as yet had sufficient time to elevate himself above the status of a slave that he may secure the means adequate to the proper care of his person and his home. As a common laborer starting life anew in the midst of his so-called superiors, he has had to look out for his own hygiene and that of his employer at the same time. The Negro woman in the home of a white family becomes responsible for getting rid of the filth of the whole group and in addition that of her own household. After toiling during the day for the means of subsistence, she has not sufficient energy on returning home at night to do for her own family what she has been employed to do for another during the day. It will not cause surprise then that such a servant becomes a germ carrier, because what microbes she does not pick up in the home of the white employer she will, no doubt, because of the neglected condition of her own family, find at home.

This situation is aggravated too by the result of race prejudice throughout the United States manifested in the conscious and unconscious segregation of the Negroes in a district not unlike that of the ghetto of the Middle Ages. Throughout the South and in most parts of the North there is an unwritten law that Negroes must not live in that part of the town in which the whites reside. This segregation makes it convenient for the municipal officials to direct their attention primarily to those portions of the city in which the leading white citizens live and to neglect that assigned to the Negroes. Traveling through the cities of the United States, one can easily discover the section in which the Negroes live even should he not see a black face. The streets are not usually paved and, if so, they are neglected; the district is seldom clean; playground and park facilities are not provided; school houses are inadequate or dilapidated; and, worst of all, into this district the city generally crowds all of its saloons and vice resorts, which, although in the Negro district of the city, are maintained not necessarily for Negroes but in many cities mainly for whites.

The Negro has been charged also with the habit of drunkenness. Reformers have looked upon the decline of the liquor traffic as the salvation of the race. No defense for the Negro in this respect should be made, but a fair-minded man will hardly take the position that the movement instituted against the use of alcohol resulted largely from the injury it has been to the Negro race. Few white persons will think that the prejudice now obtaining in this country would permit a man of his station to have so much interest in the black race. Moreover, statistics show that there are in the South many counties in which practically no Negroes at all reside and in which the movement against the liquor traffic has received its greatest impetus.

Ostensibly the Negro manifests more greed for alcohol than the white man. As a mater of fact, however, the two races are about the same in this respect. The white man is in better circumstances to provide himself with supplies of liquors at home, whereas the Negro of limited income must frequent the saloons to refresh himself from day to day. In the city of Washington during the three or four months immediately preceding the dray law now in vogue in the District of Columbia, a large number of the richest white people in the city had alcohol drinks shipped in large quantities: some of them received twenty-five, fifty, or a hundred cases of drinks and other casks of whisky.

There are in the city of Washington scores of white men who have enough whisky to supply themselves for the next twenty years. The Negro, on the other hand, having not sufficient money thus to supply his wine closet, had to make more frequent visits to the nearby cities or had to run the risk of repairing to the bootleggers for their daily or weekly supplies. This in itself, of course, became a matter of public disgrace in the eyes of the citizenry at large.

It should be said to the credit of the Negro, however, that the thousands of those who have engaged in securing these supplies of whisky followed in the footsteps of white men who engaged in the trade to amass fortunes during these closing days of the whisky regime. A considerable number of such Negroes too were sent, not to secure whisky for themselves, but for their white employers. During the last days of the whisky rule, fine-looking white women apparently of the aristocratic class joined the bootlegging brigade crowding the trains with their suitcases and their servants to stock their homes against any contingency. In numerous raids made by the police to discover supplies and the sale of liquors, they have often found the Negro and the white man working together. In many other cases they have immediately found clues to the guilt of white men for whom the Negroes have endangered their liberty to secure whisky. The Negro then belonging to the servant class has to bear the blame of the white man for whom he has served.

The Negro too is charged with the affliction of venereal diseases, a thing which now claims the attention of the reformers who in the study of the popularization of eugenics are trying to remake the race. The statistics of the United States army show that venereal diseases are more prevalent among Negroes than among whites. It is not to be concluded, however, that every Negro or every other Negro is afflicted with some sort of venereal disease. Too often we have found that a physician in the army, making an examination of a regiment of Negroes, has found an unusually large percentage of them afflicted with these diseases and he immediately generalizes on his data published to the world to advertise the shortcomings of the whole race. Some other surgeon who has examined a Negro regiment and found such little evidence of this infection can on the contrary contend that the Negroes are generally free from these diseases. This was the case with reference to Negroes who were trained for officers in the camp at Fort Des Moines during the first year of our participation in the World War.

There has not yet been brought forth any evidence to show that the Negroes are more susceptible to venereal diseases than the whites. As a matter of fact, these diseases belong to the white race. They come to the natives of the heathen world along with the Christian civilization. The natives of Africa knew nothing of these afflictions which have so handicapped the white man until the European nations brought them to Africa in the course of their great commercial expansion which resulted in the enslavement of the Negro for exploitation purposes in the world.

These venereal diseases of the white man, therefore, are more ravaging among Negroes than among whites, who during the centuries that they have been thus afflicted have developed in the course of time a bodily resistance by which immunization takes place in many members of their group. For the same reason, the Negro readily yields to the attacks of tuberculosis, another white man's disease. Other instances of this working of the law of nature appear in the hookworm and the smallpox. The hookworm has been in the Negro race for centuries and the disease does not fatally affect some members of this group, whereas a white man attacked with it easily succumbs. Smallpox among the Filipinos has been their lot so long that they have become as indifferent toward it as America is toward the whooping-cough, but a white man coming into contact with the native thus mildly attacked contracts a fatal disease.

Improvement in this respect, however, is large-ly a task of education. It has been shown that in those communities where the Negroes are well educated the percentage of those afflicted with venereal diseases is very small and that in sections where they have been neglected, where their opportunities for betterment have been poor, the percentage runs higher. Statistics show too that Negroes living in the more advanced centers of culture of the United States, as for example in the North, have so far removed themselves from this affliction that they show a smaller percentage than the educated white people of the South. It is, therefore, a result of ignorance and its eradication will depend on the extent to which the race can be generally educated to the point of realizing the awful results from these plagues.

The trouble seems to be then that the white man who brought the Negro these diseases has been at fault in not adequately informing him about the recent discoveries of the awful consequences resulting from not taking the proper steps to eradicate them. To supply this need, the professional Negroes throughout the country have organized to inform their fellow men to remove this lethargic attitude towards a condition which, if not properly handled, will result in untold injury to the race. Their efforts have recently taken the form of Health Week, instituted by Dr. Booker T. Washington and now regarded throughout the country as a season for unselfish and noble service on behalf of

a struggling people and by the people themselves as a
period in which they derive both benefit and pleasure
from contributing in a material way to their own good.

The Negro is charged too as being irreligiously
religious. He is said to emphasize the emotional rather
than the ethical side of religion. It has been said that he
feels right but does wrong, for no effort has been made
to connect character with religion. A Negro, it is said,
can do almost anything he desires but periodically he
works himself up to the point of feeling that he is all
right, that he owns this world and will take heaven
by storm, since a little talk with Jesus will make it all
right. Many preachers themselves, the leaders of the
race, those who stand above and beyond all others in
the estimation of the Negroes, are greatly at fault in
this respect. They have too often used their position
of influence as a means to exploit the virtue of their
women and the pockets of their parishioners. It is very
difficult to find a minister who has not been branded
as being a little crooked in handling the finances of
his church or in his connection with the women of his
congregation. These ministers unfortunately too have
the largest following. It seems that the worse they are,
the more people they have to harm.

Unfortunately, too, most Negro preachers are not
farsighted. They generally have that vainglorious ambition to seem rather than be and to wrest from their

congregations funds for expensive clothing, automobiles, and churches. Little effort is made to enlighten their communicants as to the solution of the economic problems of life. It seems to be sufficient for them to bury their money in unprofitable church property which can never yield any return to the race. When we bring the other wealth owned by the Negroes and their church property into comparison with similar items of the white race, the Negroes spend about twenty times as much on their churches as whites.

In spite of this imperfect emotional religion, however, the Negroes have been inclined to think that this will after all be the solution of their abstruse problem, the panacea for all their ills. They declare that the affliction of the Negroes in this country and abroad has resulted from the fact that they have strayed afar from God, and when they have once realized the evil of their ways and returned to worship God as they should, they will thereby heal their backsliding and will find themselves favored of God again. The preachers still contend that righteousness exalteth a nation and sin is a reproach to any people, but they have not as yet figured out exactly what righteousness is. It has been a sort of a blind effort in the dark, a general proclamation intended to cover a number of things intangible and which in the end does not produce the desired results.

The Negroes have not yet realized that the kind of religion worth having is that religion which by connecting with this life will prepare one for a better state not necessarily altogether of the other world. Religion should begin with men and conditions as they now are and apply common-sense principles in making them what they ought to be, a religion which takes into consideration all things influencing the future of men for good and directly promoting those things so as indirectly to promote religion and morals in all one's activities.

A few of the Negro preachers have reached this stage and are organizing what is known as institutional churches. Among these are the institutional church of the Reverend H. H. Proctor of Atlanta, Georgia, and a similar organization of the Reverend W. N. DeBerry of Springfield, Massachusetts. Proctor, a Congregational minister, practically converted his church into an organization of such groups as the day nursery, kindergarten, gymnasium, school of music, employment bureau, and Bible school. The pastor of a Congregational church, DeBerry has probably solved the problem about as well as any of these workers. In the first place, the church has a well-equipped modern plant so beautifully located and managed as to attract large numbers. It has, moreover, a parish home for working girls and a branch church at

Amherst, Massachusetts. In the main plant are maintained a free employment bureau, a women's welfare league, a night school of domestic training, and a girls' and a boys' club emphasizing the handicrafts, music, and athletics. This church has solved the problem of supplying the needs of the people during the week as well as their spiritual needs on Sunday, by emphasizing some life activity for every day in the week. Other ministers of the gospel, who have not seen fit to carry out in their parishes in such detail the establishment of social welfare work, have nevertheless done much along special lines to socialize their churches. One hears of that indefatigable worker, the Rev. Mr. Bradby, of Detroit; E. W. Bagnali, the rector of the Episcopal Church of the same city; the fearless George Frazier Miller, an Episcopal rector of Brooklyn; the talented leader, Dr. W. H. Brooks of New York City; the popular western worker, Dr. S. W. Bacote of Kansas City; Dr. J. M. Riddle of Pasadena, California; and Dr. W. H. Jernagin, of Washington, D. C. Others of this group are Dr. Richard Carroll of Greenville, South Carolina; Bishop Sampson Brooks, as pastor of the Bethel Methodist Episcopal Church in Baltimore; Dr. W. D. Johnson of Plains, Georgia, now a bishop of his denomination; the picturesque pulpit orator and beautiful word painter, Dr. Peter James Bryant, of Atlanta, Georgia; and that popular preacher of the social gospel, Dr. W. W. Browne, of the Metropolitan Baptist Church in New York City.

The very departments of these organizations will indicate the method of attack. They have in connection with these churches an employment bureau, gymnasium, library, school for instruction in manual arts, boys' and girls' club, debating society, and dramatic society, classes in social hygiene, and a visitor or social worker to report upon conditions in the homes of the poor.

This failure to look out for a man in this life is an unfortunate situation in the Negro church at the very time when the white man has an entirely different attitude toward religion. Few white people now think of a hereafter in the sense of men living on a beautiful island of by-and-by or being doomed to torment in a lake that burns with fire and brimstone. They no longer have the former conception of God, the indulgent Father, which they engrafted upon the minds of the Negroes first brought to this country. God in the mind of the white man is his race. His race is supreme and absolute among the other races of the world. One would inquire: Where is their Christianity? Where is their regard for the brotherhood of man and fatherhood of God? These principles with them are things of the past. The white people believe in a new theology, which has for its main tenet the principle that, if there

is a conflict between the interests of the white race and
the teachings of Christ, the interests of the white race
must stand first. The Negro unfortunately knows too
little of the social revolution which has taken place in
the world, if he fails to understand this situation and
to conduct himself accordingly.

The Negro has made another mistake in depending too much on politics. That the Negroes in this
country should adopt this unsatisfactory method for
the solution of their problems, however, is no surprise.
In the American frontier democracy radically distinguished from the status of the third estate in Europe,
the proletariat learned to appreciate the exercise of the
functions of citizenship as the greatest boon to life, the
thing so long withheld from him by the crowned heads
and the nobility of Europe. The poor whites, even in
America, had to struggle for centuries so to remake
governments in America as to transfer this agent of
the state to the will of the majority. And it was not
until the Civil War, the factor in bringing about this
social and political revolution for the Negroes, that the
poor whites became a factor in the affairs of the body
politic. In the proportion then that the whites emphasized the value of this privilege of voting and holding
office the Negroes learned to covet them. When freed,
therefore, they believed as so many poor whites had
done that when they succeeded in securing the ballot

and obtaining access to the public office, all of their problems would be solved, for the government can make great men and provide money and means for the support of them.

During the Reconstruction period, then, the attention of the Negroes was primarily directed to politics. For a number of years they figured conspicuously as the dominant factor in the politics of the South. The experience they had there in connection with the carpet-bag regime was both exhilarating and misleading. What was done shortly after the Civil War to elevate them to this status, they did not understand could, in a few years, be undone by the swinging of the pendulum the other way. They do not now realize that worthwhile political forces must have a broad and deep foundation in things intellectual and economic. The poor whites have recently learned that while the proletariat can destroy what these forces have established during years, it cannot rebuild, and as the thought was driven home during the World War, a prosperous country after all will be controlled, must be controlled, by the men who own the wealth of the country. The participation of the Negro in politics, therefore, while it has been and must be desirable, is, because of the results expected therefrom, a departure from the true way to success and achievement.

It is unfortunate that a large number of Negroes still stake the rise or fall of their affairs on the fortunes of one party. Most Negroes are still Republicans, and as long as the Democratic party is controlled by the advanced agents of caste and segregation, they will for some time remain so, but it is a mistake on the part of the Negroes to think that a majority of the people can be brought around to the point of thinking as Vardaman, Blease, and Hoke Smith do.[1] A majority of the people in this country, whether Republicans or Democrats, are still susceptible to reason and will hardly permit the country for a very long while to follow the fortunes of those prices of mediaeval methods. It has to some extent been fortunate for the Negroes that the Democrats have controlled the United States government during the last eight years. It has been sufficient to convince the blacks that they can in some way live during a Democratic administration. There have been many proposals for the extension of measures of Jim Crowism and to some extent has been carried out in the departments of the civil service in Washington, but on the whole, the change in the administration has not resulted in the disaster which so many of the Negroes thought would follow.

This should be sufficient to disabuse the minds of the Negroes of the thought that they can by their attachment to any particular party solve their problems. Neither party is interested in social justice. Both are trying to use the government for the good of the machines. Negroes should direct their attention to larger problems of life which when properly solved will take care of the Negroes' political and civil rights. Ordinary common sense should be sufficient for one to understand that a racial group numbering about one-tenth of the population of a large country can never hope to gain anything by constructing and carrying out a policy intended to influence the whole country to do special things on its behalf. Only so far as the Negro can connect his needs with the socialistic and economic forces now effecting the reconstruction of the world can the race claim any consideration from the public. The world is too large and too busy to stop to consider the special needs of a people who have only one or two avenues out of a difficult situation.

Notes

1   James Vardaman, Hoke Smith, and Cole Blease were leading white nationalists from Mississippi, Georgia, and South Carolina, respectively. James Vardaman served as governor of Mississippi and as a United States senator. It was Vardaman who, upon arriving in Washington, pressed the Woodrow Wilson administration to segregate blacks who worked for the federal government. Smith was at the center of whipping up the mob that caused the Atlanta Riot of 1906. Cole Blease was a senator from South Carolina who notoriously defended lynching as a defense of white womanhood. See William F. Holmes, *The White Chief: James Kimble Vardaman* (Baton Rouge: Louisiana State University Press, 1970); Dewey W. Grantham, *Hoke Smith and the Politics of the New South* (Baton Rouge: Louisiana State University Press, 1967); and Bryant Simon, "The Appeal of Cole Blease of South Carolina: Race, Class, and Sex in the New South," *The Journal of Southern History* 62 (February 1996), 57-86.

Scurlock Studio Collection, Archive Center, National Museum of American History, Smithsonian Institution

In 1921, when Woodson wrote "A Case for the Negro," he turned 46. He was six years into his career as Director of the Association for the Study of Negro Life and History (ASNLH), and had recently established his publishing house, The Associated Publishers. The original plan agreed upon by Jesse Moorland, Channing Tobias, and Woodson was for the book to be published by The Association Press, the publishing arm of the Young Men's Christian Association. Woodson later recalled that the two men disliked his treatment of black ministers, and asked him not to go forward with the book.

Jesse E. Moorland (above) and Channing Tobias (next page), two prominent leaders of the Colored YMCA movement, approached Carter G.
Woodson and implored him to write a rebuttal to a book published
by Willis D. Weatherford, *Present Forces of Negro Progress*. The two
men were so agitated by Weatherford's work of liberal racism because
he was their colleague in the YMCA movement. As the first secretary-
treasurer of the Association for the Study of Negro Life and History,
Moorland knew Woodson well enough to convince him to write a work
prompted by racial politics.

Channing Tobias is today an almost forgotten leader. In addition to working to build the black YMCA movement, Tobias directed the Phelps-Stokes Fund, became chairman of the board of directors of the National Association for the Advancement of Colored People, participated in President Truman's race relations commission, and later served as alternate representative to the United Nations. In the 1930s, Woodson revealed that Tobias and Moorland once informed him that Weatherford refused to dine with black people, indicating the kind of racist treatment that led them to ask Woodson to respond.

Willis D. Weatherford, a leading Southern Progressive, was considered "a friend of the Negro race," which was a common expression during the era. Such "friends" did not necessarily believe that the races were innately equal or that blacks and whites should mix socially. Tobias and Channing were disturbed by his published views on African Americans.

Photographs from Scurlock Studio Collection, Archive Center, National Museum of American History, Smithsonian Institution.

Despite owning a publishing house, Woodson never published his defense of the race. The manuscript was discovered fifty-five years after his death in the Association files of Rayford Logan, a Howard University professor.

Woodson's Appeal reflects the World War I era. "The Negro," wrote Woodson, "loves the country and is willing not only to give it financial support but even to die for it.... On the other hand, he actually hates the gangrene jealous and clannish, autocratic Republicans and Democrats who are the same impediments to the triumph of democracy here as the Junkers were to the liberation of the peoples of Germany." Departing from his silence on politics, Woodson made clear that he had a low estimation of Taft (above, left) and Wilson (above right and below). He referred to them as as "prejudiced charlatans."

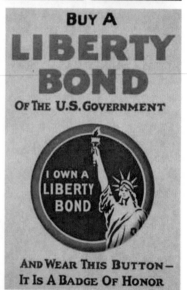

BUY A LIBERTY BOND OF THE U.S. GOVERNMENT

I OWN A LIBERTY BOND

AND WEAR THIS BUTTON— IT IS A BADGE OF HONOR

Photographs Courtesy of the Library of Congress

Courtesey of the Library of Congress

After World War I America teemed with racism and violence. Above the Klan gathers in surburban Washington, DC. Below, a black man is killed by a mob in the Chicago Race Riot.

Photograph from The Negro in Chicago, 1922.

From In the Vanguard of a Race, 1922.

A devout Christian, Woodson favored churches and ministers who promoted social services and, of course, opposed racism. Above is Rev. DeBerry of Springfield, Mass. with his staff. Below are Abbott Lyman (left) and Charles Parkhurst (right) very prominent ministers whom Woodson singled out as hypocrits for embracing segregation.

Courtesy of the Library of Congress

6

What the Negro Is Learning

The Negro was once unfortunate in his attitude toward education. In this respect he did not differ very much from the white man. The Negroes took over the antebellum white man's idea of education, which has recently disappeared among the whites. Education in the former times was largely classical because of its direct influence in preparing men for the higher pursuits of life, from which those of low estate were to be barred. Schools that were established for the education of the Negroes immediately after the Civil War, therefore, bore the stamp of European institutions of the seventeenth century. Negroes were trained away from life rather than to connect with the forces around them, to elevate themselves by elevating their fellows. This, of course, followed as a sequel to the part the Negro hoped to play in politics. The aim was to prepare all men for greatness regardless of their mental endowment. The Negro failed to realize too that the

southern white man was already running behind the
more advanced civilization of the North. Education,
therefore, became in the hands of persons thus misled
a matter of imitation considered desirable to attain a
certain ideal rather than a means of bringing out into
strength and action the powers of the mind.

A generation thereafter, Dr. Booker T. Washington came forward with a new idea, intending to bring
the race back to realization of their actual circumstances and to induce them to deal with life as it is rather
than to dream for the day that it would miraculously
become what they wanted it to be. The progress of this
education, however, apparently savored of discrimination against the Negro in that it gave the South a
chance to restrict the education of the Negro to a mere
equipment for menial service while their own youth
should receive training in literature, science, and philosophy. The shortcoming to be noted here, however,
is not that the Negro believed in any particular sort
of education, but that his attitude toward education
was utilitarian, that of getting something which would
forever secure to him the benefits which persons lacking cultural advantages could not enjoy.

Thousands of Negroes today have a different attitude. Many Negroes now study law, medicine, or
theology not to earn a living in the practice of a profession, but to make a contribution to knowledge in

these fields. Negro teachers, no longer primarily concerned with solving the problem of earning a livelihood, now undertake to serve humanity. A number of Negro students now prosecute seriously the studies which they have pursued in college, and a few of them have attained the distinction of being authorities in their chosen fields. This, of course, means more when we consider that few white Americans have been able to write a Greek grammar or construct a system of philosophy. Some Negroes have learned that excellence in the field of scholarship is one of the means by which the people of color can convince the world of their worth. It is an indirect way to attainment of the recognition and respect given a citizen. Race prejudice may be a great factor in bringing about unusual difficulties for small groups of races, but the world is not so hopelessly lost to reason as to maintain forever insurmountable barriers around a people of economic achievement and high culture.

The Negro is learning also to abandon imita-tion and blaze the way in unexplored fields. He was once afflicted with the tendency of following the well-beaten path and showed too little of the pioneering spirit. The best argument to establish this fact is the satisfaction which the Negro seemingly experienced in the South after he was liberated. Whereas there were thousands and even millions of Europeans of low estate who severed their connections with their homes in Europe to establish themselves beyond the frontier of civilization in the United States, the Negroes remained contented on the plantations where they had been impressed into the service of a superior race to do the work of hewers of wood and drawers of water. Why did the Negroes not go west and take up the arid land which was later preempted by southern Europeans? Was it the lure of politics in the South which attracted them or which invited them to stay as Frederick Douglass advised, thinking that they as a majority or large minority in that country would accordingly wield political power? Or was it that they were ignorant of the world without and could not see their opportunities in this land of possibilities within their reach? Both of these factors had much to do with the decision which governed the freedmen during the first years following the emancipation.

Yet it must not be said that the Negro race is not pioneering. It could not be expected that immediately after the Civil War the freedmen who had gone through two and a half centuries of slavery, crushing in them every tendency to take the initiative, could do other than fail to manifest a pioneering spirit at that time. One would have to establish the fact that the Negroes throughout Africa generally lacked this characteristic before the race could be generally condemned. As history shows that the Negroes of Africa as builders of civilizations have in their time passed through the same stages of development experienced by China, India, Mesopotamia, Greece, and Rome, no such charge can be placed to their account.

The reason why the Negro did not learn a better method than imitation lay in the institution of slavery. It was inevitable that persons unable to think for themselves would follow the fortunes of those who were better developed. No one can blame a slave for the failure to start out for new opportunities in the wilderness immediately after being liberated on the plantation from which he had never been permitted to go a score of miles during his whole life. Most slaves, moreover, were kept in the depths of ignorance, and especially as to the facts of geography. They not only could not read but were not permitted to master such simple facts as the cardinal points. The only way that many of them could figure out the direction in which to travel was that they had learned to follow the North Star.

Fortunately now, however, there are few Negroes dependent upon somebody else to do their thinking despite the fact that the enemies of the race have tried to take over this task. The tendency of the white men to raise up for the race certain spokesmen styling themselves leaders has been a bold effort to prevent this development of the Negro mind. Every white man has implicit confidence in some one Negro, who may be either an intelligent man or the most ignorant man of the community, but whatever his mental development or character may be, the white man concerned will not pay attention to the words or the warning of any other man of color. This Negro then is the one whose advice all should heed and whose example all should emulate.

Out of this state of affairs develops then the so-called Negro leader. With their minds thus molded, the Negroes have accepted the head man or the leader as a necessity in their civilization, and they usually follow the fortunes of such. That a race under such circumstances should often run against rocks should not excite surprise, for a large group of people depending on any one person for advice or direction along all lines must find themselves finally misinformed and misled. The white people of the United States, for example, would be in an awful plight if the whole one hundred million depended solely on the words or the dictation of one man, whether he be Cole Blease or Charles William Eliot.[1] Negroes now feel that no one man is capable of doing the thinking for the whole race.

The Negro is too learning to use proper methods to set his case before the world. The race formerly relied too much on mere agitation. A man striking him a blow or insulting his wife was prosecuted only to the extent that the unfortunate Negro would call together his friends in a corner too far away for his antagonist to hear the proceedings and pass resolutions to the effect that he was not properly treated. A community would rise up against a Negro and drive him out, and he would merely send to the authorities, who have winked at the very act, a protest from an indignation meeting for a redress of the grievance.

How different is the attitude of the Negro of to-day! Like other oppressed races the Negro is learning to strike back. The Negro observes that one seldom hears of an indignation meeting held among the Jews but frequently learns of their many wrongs being righted. Some years ago a newspaper in one of the large cities became antagonistic in its attitude toward the Hebrews. A short while thereafter they purchased this newspaper and it is now singing their praises. The Japanese, another race persecuted on the Pacific coast, did not generally advertise their meetings intended to devise schemes for the redress of their grievances but to influence public opinion. The 10,000 Japanese in San Francisco established two daily newspapers of eight pages each. Negroes have, therefore, during recent years learned the power of the press. They have established and well supported a number of scientific and popular magazines, published a score of widely circulated weeklies, and have now two dailies which bid fair to wield a tremendous influence in securing recognition for the Negro race.

This general progress has meant an increasing interest in movements instituted to right the wrongs of the race. Negroes of the more radical reform type and sympathetic white persons cooperating with them have at times been discouraged by the apparent apathy of the Negroes for their own cause. In recent years, however, the spread of new ideas as to natural rights and democracy has been so general that movements to secure the Negroes the full enjoyment of their civil and political rights have not lacked support. This work has been undertaken by several national organizations, some of which have not been well managed. One of them, however, the National Association for the Advancement of Colored People, has through its live branches in all parts of the country decidedly solidified the race against the aggressions of caste and bids fair to develop into a strong political organization.

These movements, moreover, are no longer the empty protest of the emotional element. Indignation meetings of the old order, to be sure, are held throughout the country, but some of them are productive of desirable results. In contradistinction to such assemblies of long ago, the people in attendance unstintingly contribute money for the promotion of specific causes

and willingly pay annual membership fees to maintain
the organization. The National Association for the
Advancement of Colored People has a membership of
50,000, publishes the *Crisis*, a monthly magazine with
a circulation of 100,000, and is now raising a fund of
$50,000 to exterminate lynching. Its goal is worldwide
democracy, its watchword is equality and justice, and
its constituency embraces all men of sufficient culture
to be above the barbarous procedure of kith and kin
justice and to believe in liberty for all mankind.

The Negro has learned also to appreciate the value
of the truth. During the days of slavery the white men
relied upon his ability to mislead the Negroes through
falsehoods mainly intended to destroy their confidence
in one another to prevent them from securing racial
cooperation. By various fabrications the Negroes of
one plantation were taught that the bondmen of another hated them, and by similar methods the slaves
were thus arrayed against the free Negroes. This training unfortunately left on the Negro mind a mark which
has been difficult of eradication even among Negroes
who are generally well-informed. A demonstration of
this recently occurred in Washington, where almost
the whole community became unnecessarily stirred up
by a false rumor as to immoral practices in the Negro
public schools merely because one teacher was known
to be indirectly connected with the exploits of a white

moral pervert who was making some incursions into circles of undesirable people of color. Men of the city who should have had a little judgment believed these rumors. Unprincipled lawyers in hope of obtaining fees and grafting preachers in quest of a collection held mass meetings periodically throughout the city. Speeches were made from which came accounts circulated by a few hard-up starvation-fighting Negro newspapers to scandalize five hundred women whose Christian character, superior culture, and unselfish service rank them among the most desirable women of the world.

The thinking class of Negroes, however, far outnumber these emotional mischief makers. In Washington, the same city in which a thousand dollars was raised to spread a scandal, a fund of thousands of dollars was collected to fight segregation and stamp out lynching. The Negroes as a group have learned to curb these mischief makers and to use the tractability of the race for more desirable purposes. The orator without deeds, the promoter without a cause, and the agitator without a desirable objective can no longer sway large masses of Negroes. The Negroes now realize how often they have been misled by persons desiring to reach selfish ends, and it is now difficult to array a large number of them against one of their own. The tendency of recent years has been to regard the faults and shortcomings in the race itself far less menacing than the attacks of the enemy from without, and it is to this end that a large majority of the Negroes are directing their efforts, and it is for this purpose that the race is now being rapidly solidified throughout the country.

While it is to the credit of the Negro that he is not vindictive, he is learning not so easily to forget the insults forced upon him. It used to be that the white man who wronged a black man one day might with very little effort the following day readjust matters and make him feel that he is his friend. The Negro would go into a drug store where the proprietor would refuse to sell him a drink of soda water because of its meaning as a step towards social equality, but from that same man he would buy drugs. The department stores in the South which refused to permit Negroes to try on clothing found that they did not lose their patronage and that they often willingly purchase their goods on disadvantageous terms fixed by the proprietor. In many of the southern cities, stores running a credit business depend largely on the trade of Negroes. Moreover, these establishments were able to hold their patrons in spite of the fact that their collectors in making their rounds during the week insulted and in some instances even beat women who were unable to make the required partial payments.

To overcome some of these things and do for themselves what others cannot do for them, the Negroes have learned more about organization in the business world. Generally speaking, the Negro has about as much wealth as the average white man. The difference has been that the whites learned to pool their capital with a view of establishing businesses and promoting enterprises which will confer benefits upon the whole group. Because Negroes lack confidence in their own men who are actually doing something to rise in the business world and because of the fond attachment to white men in business of long standing, it has been difficult to develop in certain parts of the South a sufficient number of Negro businessmen to relieve the race of insult.

It is very encouraging, however, to know that during recent years there has been a tendency among the Negroes to rid themselves of this fault and enterprising men of color have been encouraged and supported sufficiently to rise high in the business world. The race may well point with pride to the fifty banks and other such establishments and especially the Providential Association of Greensboro, North Carolina; the Richmond Beneficial Insurance Company; the National Benefit Association of Washington; the Standard Life Insurance Company of Atlanta, Georgia; the Whitelaw Apartment House Corporation of Washington; Poro

College, a chemical firm in St. Louis; the Madame C. J. Walker establishment in New York; and the Brown and Stevens firm in Philadelphia.[2] In view of this unusual development of the Negro in business with the requirements for supplying almost any need in the community it is becoming unpopular for any member of the race to withhold his support from the Negro in business. Not that the Negro has reached the stage of clannishness, but that he has been thoroughly convinced of the ability of his fellow sufferer successfully to compete with others and he is willing to give him the same support he would to any other businessman from whom no better terms may be obtained.

Notes

1   Woodson compares the demagogue Senator Cole Blease of South Carolina with Charles Eliot, the scientist and president of Harvard University, his alma mater.

2   The Richmond Beneficial Insurance Company has records in the archives and special collections of Virginia Commonwealth University. Woodson had more to say about the history of black insurance companies. See James L. Conyers, ed. *Carter G. Woodson: A Historical Reader* (New York: Garland Publishing, 2000), pp. 108-128. Useful information on many of the firms mentioned in the text can be found in the *Encyclopedia of African American Business History*, edited by Juliet E. K. Walker (New York: Greenwood Press, 1999) and in A'Lelia Bundles, *On Her Own Ground: The Life and Times of Madam C. J. Walker* (New York: Scribner, 2001).

7

Superior Qualities of the Negro

Nothing exhibits more forcefully the Negro's claim to superiority than his cheerfulness. Dark as the hour has at times seemed, the Negro has never lost hope. In the midst of his trials he has calmed the fears of his fellows, mustered up the courage of a pioneer, and boldly faced the ordeals of a hostile environment. When others thus situated would consider all as lost, the Negro gives the smile of sunshine, manifests the humor of the philosopher, and sings the song prophetic of triumphant victory. How the Negro has under adverse circumstances maintained this attitude toward his oppressors, how he can be so sanguine, has evoked the admiration of all men. Some have undertaken to explain this attitude as the Negro's ignorance of his situation and his failure to appreciate the serious problems which an impending crisis may forebode. When, however, we observe the same characteristics in Negroes who have been educated in the best schools and have come up under the influence of radical race leadership, the investigator must find some other answer to his inquiry.

The Negro must be lauded also for his unusual gratitude. A study of mankind shows that many races have not yet attained the stage of freedom from the sin of ingratitude. But the Negro has been enabled to win friends because of his heart-felt appreciation of efforts put forth in his behalf. Philanthropists who first directed their attention to the Negro with stinted support have been encouraged to do so much more for the race than they originally planned. Northern and Southern white friends, who have suffered social proscription in overriding the barriers of race prejudice, have found their greatest reward in the Negro's appreciation of what they have said and done on his behalf.

The Negro is superior to the other races also in that although he does not soon forget the good which one does him, he more quickly forgets an effort to do him an injury. He has all but lived up to the principles of malice toward none and charity for all. This has been regretted by a number of Negroes and even the whites as a weakness rather than a virtue of the Negro. Such persons have hopes that the Negro will learn to resent more of the insults and avenge more of the wrongs done to him. Negroes too have at times lost

their control and tried to right their own wrongs, as
recently manifested in the case of the Houston riot.
The large majority of Negroes, however, still forgive
and forget. It is due, I believe, to this characteristic
alone that the Negro race has been able to endure in
the midst of the hostile men. In the course of time the
unfriendly relations now existing between the two
races in this and other countries will be adjusted and
the Negro will come into his own; but had the Negro
taken the attitude of bold defense assumed by the
American Indian, he would have likewise suffered
extermination.

The Negro, moreover, is naturally philanthropic. Most of what the race through its separate organizations has achieved has been made possible by
its philanthropy. If ill-disposed school officials in a
community fail to provide facilities of education for
Negro youth, a progressive leader may raise money
to conduct a subscription school.In localities where
Negroes suffer from the invidious distinction of differences in pay for teachers, Negro patrons very often
increase the teachers' income by contributions. In the
support of their churches they have been too generous. During the last fifty years they have accumulated
more than $100,000,000 worth of church property.
They maintain their pastors in luxury and ease and
support, through the church as an agency, institutions

established to help the poor and especially organized to promote the higher education of the Negroes. According to recent reports, the Negroes annually contribute $1,000,000 in this way to their own education.

Among the superior qualities of the Negro should be mentioned also his patience. He has been within the reach of opportunity and has been forced to realize the fact that the door through which he must pass to avail himself of it is shut, but he does not feel that this condition of affairs will always obtain. He is then willing patiently to wait until his time may come. Today, as in the days of slavery, the Negroes believe that there is a way out of their difficulties and that the divinity shaping the destinies of nations will eventually bring to pass a change in the order of things. The Negro will, therefore, work and await results. This is not the attitude of the lazy man. It is rather the position taken by those who endeavor to put forth efforts expected of a struggling people believing that unselfish and unceasing service must have in the end the desired results. History does not show such long suffering of a people so generally afflicted with the scorn of races availing themselves of the opportunity to degrade and to crush a group among them branded as inferior largely because of a difference in color.

The blacks are superior to the whites in that they are more religious. It must be admitted that many

Negroes are more superstitious than religious, but in holding on to religion until a more forceful factor for inhibition can be developed, the Negroes have thereby maintained a system which serves them as a moral police force. Negroes generally accept the Bible in word and spirit. They do not always live up to its principles, but it serves as a guide and at the same time constitutes the goal to which the multitude must aspire. Persons who think little of the Biblical doctrine and fail to support the church are never influential among Negroes. Ninety-five percent of the Negroes in the professions belong to some church. The belief in the doctrines that one will reap what he sows and that the evildoer will be afflicted with punishment after death serves as such a restraint among the blacks that the majority of them are wisely conservative in dealing with their oppressors. It would be difficult to imagine exactly how the racial conflict would have worked out in this country if the Negro, like the white man, had abandoned this sort of religion without accepting some other system to secure restraint.

There is little doubt that this religious nature of the Negro has been most effective in making the blacks generally conservative. The Negro is almost too devoted to tradition. He believes in progress, but when he has time to think, it is difficult to convince him that he should be the first by whom the new thing should be tried when he has many reasons for being attracted to the old. Some thoughtless Negroes have been easily misled by persons playing upon their emotions, but these same Negroes are just as easily disillusioned when they have the opportunity to learn the truth. There have been few instances, therefore, of Negroes abandoning any cause, leader, or institution which has in time promoted their welfare.

The Negro, therefore, is a law-abiding citizen. This may sound like strange doctrine to the Negro hater who has never heard of the Negro other than as a criminal. The reason one hears of so many offenses of the Negro is that the Negro is not adjudged according to the law of civilized nations, but according to the will of white men dominant in that particular community. Moreover, the very deed which makes a Negro a criminal makes a white man a hero. To kill a Negro is the duty of every aggrieved white man. To inconvenience or anger a white man is just cause for the death of a Negro. Violating the law is the prerogative of the white. The thought of the oppressor is that this is a white man's country and if the Negro stays here he must be perfect.

It is exceedingly difficult for a Negro not to commit so-called crime. In many parts of this country it is a crime for a Negro to go into a city park, use a public lavatory, drink from a public fountain, take a seat in a hotel, eat in a café, use a public elevator, walk on the sidewalk, ride in a Pullman sleeper, sit near a white person in a streetcar, or sit anywhere when a white person is standing. In such communities a Negro is not allowed to dispute a white man's word, must go when the white man tells him to move, and must not be seen in certain parts unless there in the capacity of a servant. Where these "offences" are not prohibited by statute, a Negro disregarding these unwritten laws is usually beaten by a white man or an officer bringing him into court to be punished on a charge fabricated to suit the occasion, branding the Negro in question as a desperado and the like whether he be a man of culture or not.* Negroes in the employ of certain whites cannot contend for what belongs to them when an effort

---

* The experience of Dr. J. I. Johnson, now Minister to Liberia, is a case in evidence. While teaching in an Ohio town not far from Cincinnati, he crossed the Ohio in Covington, Kentucky, to visit some friends. On returning in a crowded streetcar, two white men came in and stood over him, expecting that he, being a Negro, would give one of them his seat. As he failed to do this, one of the white men began to comment on the undesirable changes in Negroes now in that they do not know their places and the like and proceeded to discuss how he and his friends in Georgia disposed of Negroes who did not respect a white man any more than to sit while he is standing. Not being able to restrain himself any longer Dr. Johnson said: "As I am the only colored man in the car, I take it for granted that you are talking about me." Thereupon the imposter swore at Johnson, using unusually foul language. Johnson then leaped upon him and handled him rather roughly for a few minutes, but upon realizing that he was about to be mobbed in Kentucky, he escaped through the crowd, took another car and crossed the river into Ohio. That day the Cincinnati Enquirer appeared with bold headlines portraying in the usual style the assault of a burly Negro on a gentleman from Georgia and lamenting the fact that the country could not rid itself of such undesirables.

is made to cheat them. They cannot under penalty of serious injury leave the service of such cruel employers, and often those not desirous of hiring themselves out are impressed into the service of wicked taskmasters. How the Negroes, thus encompassed by so many mediaeval restrictions, have not according to the white man's reckoning a higher record for criminality than is commonly reported is a mystery of modern times. It is remarkable that ninety-nine percent of the Negroes are not on this basis branded as criminals. That they are not is eloquent proof that the Negro race is the most law-abiding people known to history.

In meeting the greatest of all tests the Negro decidedly surpasses his white brother in loyalty. In the days of his ignorance in slavery when his mental development had not extended far enough to inculcate a deep appreciation of the love of country, he manifested his loyalty to his master and to his plantation. Southern leaders are still talking of the fidelity of the Negroes during the Civil War, when they protected the wives of their masters who were at the front fighting to defend the cause of the Confederacy, established to perpetuate an institution which debased the blacks to the plane of beasts and doomed them to benighted darkness. These leaders rue the day when these pleasant relations were broken up by the emancipation of the race. They fail to see how this same loyalty has developed in a broader sense into a characteristic far superior to that of fidelity to one's master or interest in one's peculiar locality. In the Negro of today this feeling is patriotism, loyalty to the flag, the willingness to bare his breast to the bullet and offer himself as a sacrifice on the altar of his country. The unreconstructed Confederates, still handicapped by sectionalism, cannot appreciate this broad vision and extended development of the Negro mind, which, in spite of difficulties, has experienced an evolution, to reach which the whites will, as present circumstances indicate, have to spend years in development.

When the call to the colors came to the Southerners during the World War, instead of responding as a citizenry should, all sorts of excuses were offered to evade the responsibility of sending their sons to the front. At the same time others were seriously objecting to the enlistment of the Negroes, believing that training in the use of arms and the service in a free country like France might, in the end, render them undesirable for living in the midst of their former conditions in the South. This meant at first then that the South was in a dilemma as to whether or not it could heartily support the war or heartily oppose it. The last impulse was to send the Negroes to be sacrificed, believing that by the recrudescence of the Ku Klux Klan, those Negroes who succeeded in returning could be prevented for self-assertion and that the whites above all would thereby be spared.

We do not mean to say here, however, that the South did not furnish a considerable number of white men. Southerners were generally drafted later when it was made clear that the war would go on and that any attempt to evade the responsibility would place that section in an embarrassing position. The records show, however, that in the proportion of their population, the Negroes sent to the front outnumbered the whites.

The loyalty of the Negroes too was borne out by their record in the support of the war. Wherever they were asked to contribute to the Young Men's Christian Association, the Red Cross, or to buy Liberty Bonds, they cheerfully responded. In several towns, by mis-understanding, Negroes raised the whole quota among themselves. In the state of North Carolina it has been shown by statistics that in practically every county that oversubscribed its quota, the percentage of the Negro population was larger than that of the general percentage of the Negro population in the state.

In spite of these facts as to superior qualities of the Negro, the average white man is of the opinion that the Negro has a feeling of inferiority in his presence. Nothing can be so far from the truth. True enough, the Negro intimidated as he has been has a feeling of fear before a man who in his imperfect state is not governed by moral law in his dealing with the helpless. The attitude of many Negroes is that they are superior in many respects to the whites who are lording it over them in such an inhuman way. They feel that they are like the innocent captives of the Greek wars impressed into the service of the barbarians of Sparta. They dare not irritate the lion when the head of the innocent is in his mouth, but they do not feel that in character and moral fibre the beast is superior to his victim.

The white man believes that the Negroes consider him an example of morality. Many of them do, but the Negro race is far from making an effort at the slavish imitation of the white man's morals. Much has been said about the Negroes' indulgence in drunken brawls and their sexual looseness and the like, but almost any Negro servant working around white people and any reader of the daily papers can see the duplication of these offences in higher circles among the whites. A white man once said to the writer that men like Jack Johnson did their Negro race much harm. I agreed with him, but took occasion to say also that it is strange that the white race has not also suffered just as much from the escapades of Harry K. Thaw and H. B. Moens. While the poor Negro culprit and his termagant sweetheart are speedily sent to prison or the gallows, the white wretch of means is left to fight it out with his money in the courts until he is released as an all but martyred hero. All the while the American public delights in the theatrical feats of his companion whose illicit relations in high places make her an unusual attraction for white people of "culture."[1] With the Negro the amount of money a man has and the family or race to which he belongs does not excuse the offence as is the case with the white man. Here among the whites morality becomes a relative matter determined on the mediaeval basis by one's blood or kin or clan or race or wealth. Seeing the situation in a different light, the Negro is unable to find in the white man's code of morals anything to serve him as a guide to more righteous conduct.

There is also among the whites the belief that Negroes, because of the much advertised superiority of white women over those of color, diligently seek to associate with and marry the former. The Southern states have therefore enacted numerous laws to prevent this so-called danger to the white man's civilization. In fact, the race question in America is purely a sexual one. If the whites could countenance the legal marriages of the races, the race question would almost cease in a generation, although the one race would not for centuries, if ever, be absorbed by the other; for, as a matter of fact, the sections of the country in which intermarriage is not prohibited experience less interbreeding than the South, where it is openly practiced between the white men and colored women and only clandestinely between white women and men of color. Negroes, like any other race, have a racial instinct, and few of them are so attracted to the white race as to override that impulse in selecting a life companion.

Unlike the white man too, the Negro does not believe that money is everything, and for that reason he is unwilling to do certain things his white neighbor often does to make money. During the last fifty years the economic progress of the Negroes in America has excelled that of any other people in the world similarly circumstanced, but the accumulation of things material has not been tarnished by the stigma of cheating and graft. They have on the contrary taken advantage of the rise and fall of prices and the increment in the values of unimproved property. No one has ever heard of a Negro who went very far in cheating his own people. A few have tried it, but the antagonistic attitude toward any man known as having taken advantage of his fellows has been such that few have been able to continue such a course.

Notes

1   The ne'er-do-well, womanizing scion of a wealthy Pittsburgh family, Harry K. Thaw was involved in a love triangle with Evelyn Nesbit and the famous architect Stanford White. Thaw eventually abused, then married Nesbit and murdered White. Infamously, he was found innocent by reason of insanity. The lurid details of the affair constituted a well-known scandal of the early twentieth century and eventually became the material for novels and movies, including E. L. Doctorow's *Ragtime*. H. B. Moens tweaked anti-miscegenation proponents by introducing black women who could pass into white circles and then revealing their racial identities. An amateur anthropologist, Moens was arrested for having photographs of nude women (mulattos) in his possession. The Moens controversy is briefly treated in Pamela Haag, *Consent: Sexual Rights and the Transformation of American Liberalism* (Ithaca: Cornell University Press, 1999), p. 123, and Michael MacDonald Mooney, *Evelyn Nesbit and Stanford White: Love and Death in the Gilded Age* (New York: Morrow, 1976).

8

What the White Man Thinks of the Negro

It will be interesting, however, to know that a race possessing so many of those qualities which make it one of the most desirable of the human races has been so generally branded with marks of deficiency and inferiority. The grounds upon which the critics of the race have undertaken to base this scandal are supposedly scientific. There has been a revival of the pseudo-scientific study of the Negro during recent years. It is, however, merely the return of the antebellum political philosopher in the disguise of the trained investigator. They usually begin with the assertion that all races are not equal, and undertake to account for certain differences resulting from the African temperament of the Negro. The limited opportunity of the white man to study the Negro in Africa makes no difference in the conclusion. As a matter of fact, the majority of the libelous writers on the Negro race have never seen

Africa. They merely try to find among the Negroes in the United States certain undesirable conditions which they endeavor to explain in terms of hearsay evidence as to African life and customs. They make no effort to discover the extent to which the Negro's development in the United States has been influenced downward by the peculiar training of the Negro in slavery. Such dissertations and books must, therefore, be considered ludicrous, for they deal with results without understanding causes and are largely the opinions of enemies interested in discomfiting those struggling upward when designated to be kept down.

The Negro is commonly charged with being vain. This is accounted for by the assertion that the race is in a childlike stage when it is unable to understand values and it must, therefore, deal with things on the surface. This criticism, however, comes not from truth but from the prejudices of mediaeval times which resulted in those social distinctions that the house, the dress, and the amusements of the lord be separate and distinct from those of the serf. Even in modern Europe today one will find certain men who are tailors to aristocrats. Their garments are to be made of a special sort of cloth which must not be sold to persons of low estate. American white people inheriting these ideas bear it grievously to see a Negro man or woman living in a home or clad in clothes and shoes of the sort common among whites. Not long ago the writer happened to be on a streetcar into which came a fine-looking, well-dressed woman of color, who attracted the attention of almost every one in the car. A white woman in the crowd remarked: "That is the trouble with the Negroes now. They try to get everything white folks have."

No effort should be made to excuse any tendency of the Negro toward vanity. This is a habit among people of all races and of all conditions. It is too prevalent among Negroes, just as it is among the whites of the United States, and anything to bring the masses back to the realization of the necessity for common sense, especially in dress, will be a contribution to American civilization. Under such circumstances it is certainly natural for many Negroes to follow in the wake of those with this inordinate desire for dress and sham, but the race as a whole must not be branded as especially weak in this respect because of the unfair criticism of prejudiced white persons inveighing against it on account of their inability to bring it to pass that the life of the Negroes shall become socially different from that of the whites merely to prevent anything indicative of racial equality.

Another charge brought against the Negro is that his mind is superstitiously childlike. He lives in a land of ghosts and fairies that he considers potential factors in shaping the destinies of men. It must be admitted that the Negroes have their share of superstition, but on the other hand, it must be conceded that such was greatly accentuated by slavery itself. This superstition, as investigation has shown, was not brought over from Africa. It was an inheritance from the white man's civilization in the United States. Whereas by education and general social progress the white man has risen above it, the Negroes, in their neglected state, have departed from it less slowly. To say that such a condition obtains generally among Negroes, however, is decidedly untrue. Under educational influences the Negroes as a majority have an intelligent attitude toward life. Moreover, it is no reflection on the Negroes to speak of superstition among them, for you will find this condition obtaining among people of all conditions, of all times and everywhere. In New England today there is the same sort of superstition that one finds among the Negroes in the most backward parts of the South. People were once hanged in Boston because they were declared guilty of witchcraft.

The Negro too has been charged with being cruel. This characteristic, it is said, manifests itself in their relations among themselves and in their treatment of animals. It has been thought also that this so-called habit resulted from an African trait exhibited in the tendency of the native to indulge in all sorts of human butchery in that land. It has been asserted that during the days of slavery the Negro slave driver was often more taxing than the white overseer. The cruelty of Negroes to their children has been likewise referred to as an evidence of inferiority.

How anyone can contend, however, that the blacks are more cruel than the whites is a mystery to a thinking man. The whole history of the white race has been cruelty in the extreme, justified by its claim to be the sole representative of God in remaking the world and shaping the destinies of nations. To say nothing about the past history, if one would merely direct his attention to the present, he would find sufficient evidence to prove that the Negroes are in every respect less guilty of cruelty than the white people. Colonial expansion developing from commercial enterprises promoted by modern nations like England, Germany, and Belgium furnishes sufficient evidence to this effect. These countries have wantonly disregarded the thoughts, feelings, and aspirations of the natives in foreign lands, dispossessed them of their homes, impressed them into menial service, and have even put them to death when their exhausted condition rendered them no longer useful to their nefarious enterprises.

The world, moreover, must still cry out in horror at the mention of England in South Africa and Belgium in the Congo. In the United States, where white men are not considered so cruel to Negroes, we find to the credit of this "highly civilized" Caucasian lynchings and massacres resulting during the last fifty years in the death of 3,000 helpless Negroes, many of whom were burned at the stake. In the World War, the Germans, who before the outbreak were considered the most advanced people in modern culture, crushed babies beneath their militant tread, bludgeoned the aged from whom they could obtain no service, and violated women left defenseless by their male relatives who had gone to fight for their helpless country. They drove the poor from their homes to starve in the waste places of the military area, dropped bombs upon the wounded in hospitals, sank ships transporting unoffending neutrals, and tortured their captives to death by gouging out their eyes and cutting out their tongues. No tribe in Africa, no settlement of Negroes in any other part of the world, has ever exhibited evidences of cruelty to surpass these.

Another wrong opinion about the Negro commonly prevails. Persons interested in this race deeply regret their gregarious tendencies, which make them think of the Negroes as a loafing class. The Negroes, they observe, stop in front of the church after dismissal, loiter around their theaters before and after performances, assemble before pool rooms and saloons even when they are not participating in what is going on. In fact, they give their section of the city undue advertisement as to racial aspects by the numbers of the race thereby drawn into brawls and feats of toughs assembled by the way. On the whole it must be admitted that the Negro is at fault in assembling around public places doing nothing without purpose. Persons of influence with the masses cannot do the race a better service than to uproot this tendency, which differs so much from anything of the sort among American white people whose standard is the one by which the Negro race is measured. It is to be regretted that few Negro public men ever publicly denounce the habit.

It is a mistake, however, to think of the majority of the Negroes as a class of loafers. This habit of flocking together in places, moreover, does not necessarily mean shiftlessness. There are several reasons for this gregarious habit of the blacks. In the first place, there is the group of the unemployed. It is seldom that all men in the community can be employed and under such circumstances the Negroes must suffer, for in the apportionment of the good things of this world the Negro always comes last. Few white men will employ a Negro, if they can find a white man who will work for the same wages, and the Negroes themselves cannot take care of their unemployed. The Negro race in the United States has in fifty years made unprecedented economic progress, but the group at present is far from affording capitalists enough to make a material difference in the employment of Negroes.

Another reason for this gregariousness among Negroes is menial service, the sort of labor in which most members of the race are engaged. Menial service, being largely drudgery, does not stimulate the thinking powers of the mind and tends to keep a man as a machine to be run as long as a certain motor force is applied and to cease when that fails. A man thus employed does not have to plan and carries from his work no thought of tomorrow. He has little use for the world except so far as it appeases his hunger or furnishes his amusement. In fact, a man thus engaged needs the excitement of the group to get his mind away from the drudgery awaiting him tomorrow. If it were not for some such opportunity and the humor of the Negro to respond to it, many of them would become madmen. The experience of other races similarly situated attests to the truth of these observations.

Many Negroes crowding the street, however, belong neither to the loafing class nor to the unemployed. Some of the Negroes who roam through the city seemingly carefree work at night, and others work during the day. Many worthy Negroes, moreover, apparently loaf as a mere habit. Passing through a business street in the Negro quarter of a city not long ago, the writer saw the owner of a forty-thousand-dollar building leaning against the structure in a loafing fashion while talking to a well-to-do lawyer loitering in front of his office in the same building.

One will inquire exactly why Negroes of this type should thus stigmatize their race. The answer is easy. Places of amusement open to Negroes are few. Negroes are received in few theaters, are not wanted in clubs, have no access to all places of recreation even when maintained by the government, and are not welcomed in white churches when they have none of their own. On one occasion while visiting a city in which there were few blacks, the writer asked a Negro lawyer of the city to direct him to a church where he might worship that Sunday. The lawyer replied that he usually went to the races on Sunday, as he found the managers in charge much more hospitable and fraternal than the white churches. The writer did not witness the races, but a visit to one of the white churches convinced him that horse racing would be an unprofitable undertaking if persons frequenting race tracks were received as he was at the white church he attended in that city.

The Negroes must therefore be restricted to a few places of their own, which in time become a sort of Mecca to which they all like to go and from which they are reluctant to depart. That some of the resorts which they learn to frequent become denizens of vice follows as a sequel. The eradication of the evil, however, will not be a problem if the white man will cease circumscribing the Negro race, will liberate it socially that it may develop the power to strengthen the weak members of the group resulting from conditions beyond its control. The thought as to the Negro loafing in public places should excite sympathy rather than scorn, should enlist support rather than the antagonism of a race which has been instrumental in developing in the Negro almost every undesirable quality he has.

White men still speak of the Negro as lacking self-control. Most of the hardships imposed upon Negroes have been considered justified largely on the ground that the Negroes lack self-restraint. Unless intimidated and made to realize that he is to be confined at all times to a certain place and required to demean himself in a manner peculiar to his status, he will become a destroying factor in society. Here again the Negroes have been branded as a childlike people endeavoring to obtain certain things which if secured would be harmful. It is said that they know not how to suffer in the present to have a greater joy in the end. This so-called lack of self-restraint results, some say, from his tropical temperament. Living in a climate in which there is no struggle for life, where man, unlike the inhabitant in the temperate zones, must work one six-month period to be above want the other, the Africans have not had necessity for exercising self-control since they could easily obtain whatever they wanted. Among them there is an abundance of food and drink and an abundance of women. Sexual indulgence among them leads to a high birth rate and consequently to a high death rate.

No one will gainsay the contention that the Negro is far from being free of self-indulgence, but generally speaking he is far superior to the white man in this respect. Self-restraint, as the white man sees it, has been confined to sexual indulgence and in this respect the Negro, so far as his situation in Africa is concerned, is not inferior to that of other races similarly situated. In their condition, as in certain groups of the Caucasian races, polygamy is practiced with all of its undesirable results, but in the circle of a man's wives one finds as much loyalty to their recognized connections and as much happiness in their position as one finds among any other people handicapped by this same habit. Between the American white people and the Negroes there is no comparison. If the whites are so free from self-indulgence, how does it happen that more than one-fifth of the Negroes of the United States have an infusion of white blood?

The adverse criticism as to sexual indulgence by American white men results largely from the fact that many of the Negroes lynched in this country are charged with criminally assaulting white women. It can certainly be proved that Negroes have been guilty of these crimes and no fair-minded man will in any way condone such offenses. Few Negroes will undertake to defend such undesirable members of their group. They are rather of the opinion that the sooner that they are legally executed, the better it will be for all. On the other hand, few white men are willing to concede the fact that in many cases when Negroes are charged with criminal assault it is merely a case of careless fornication and when exposed the white woman concerned seeks to protect herself by proclaiming the charge of criminal assault.

Cases in evidence are numerous. A white minister who has worked in both Arkansas and Missouri informed the writer that in his community a Negro charged with this sort of crime was promptly lynched and the community again breathed with freedom when the culprit was no longer to menace their homes. Some years thereafter, when this white woman died, realizing that she had caused the death of an innocent man, she confessed on her deathbed that she had for years cohabited with this Negro. The writer himself lived twenty-seven miles from a Southern town in which a young man who had served as a servant in a rich family was one day supposedly caught in this same act with the cultivated daughter of his rich employer. Before he could be lynched, however, he had sufficient presence of mind to place in the hands of a distinguished white lawyer, a friend of his family, numerous letters which the young woman had written him expressing her undying devotion to him and requesting of him periodically these pleasurable visitations. When the mob was preparing to lynch the Negro, this gentleman produced these letters to show that the young man was innocent of the charge of criminal assault. The young white woman concerned went to this gentleman, begged him to give up or destroy these letters, but he persistently refused to do so. Seeing that she had been exposed and knowing the opprobrium that she would suffer thereafter, she went to a river nearby and drowned herself.

One reason for connecting the idea of criminal assault especially with the Negro is that the same crime committed by a white man is hardly reported beyond the limits of his locality. The unusual publicity given what the Negro does results not so much from the heinousness of the crime but from the revulsion of feeling at the thought that any Negro should have sexual intercourse with a white woman. It is a common occurrence for a white man to rape a woman of color, but few newspapers controlled by the whites will publish such news. About two years ago a white man criminally assaulted a woman of color within two blocks of the house of the writer, but not a newspaper in the nation's capital mentioned it. During the recent race riots in Washington, caused by the supposed criminal assaults on white women by Negroes, there were two actual cases of white men undertaking to rape women of color but not a white man would give any publicity to these facts.

Negroes in the company of their desirable-looking wives and daughters in the South are sometimes accosted and made to desert them by white wretches who try to force these women to yield to their base purposes. Under these circumstances, there are for the Negro only two alternatives—resist the wretch and die or escape and live. Women of color in the South are afraid to tell their husbands of the insults with which they meet. And husbands sometimes refrain from going on the streets with their wives, knowing that although they cannot protect their wives, they may in their anger undertake it only to see themselves killed by the mob rushing to the defense of the white culprit. And what will it matter, moreover, to take it to court? Few courts in the South would believe the Negro's story of injuring a white man to defend the sanctity of his home, and whatever the white plaintiff says is law. Negroes who harm white men by protecting their homes are promptly lynched or burned at the stake. To give the Negro home such protection, moreover, would seriously interfere with the thing fundamental in Southern civilization, namely the silent acceptance of the use of the Negro race to furnish an outlet for the vices of the libertines produced in the beautifully clean circles of the South.

9

What the Negro Is Thinking

The white man in the South either potentially or actually segregates the Negroes in his community. He does not generally have anything to do with a Negro unless he calls one for menial service or has a business transaction with him. True enough, the peddler, huckster, or collector daily comes into contact with the generality of the people of color but white men of this type do little thinking and cannot at best divine exactly what the race is about. The white man of influence, who has little contact with the representative class of Negroes, banishes the race as a whole from his thought and thinks of the group as a mass of mentally inert and psychically dead aggregate to be despised but tolerated as an iniquity visited upon the third and fourth generations.

It may be worthwhile, however, to inquire exactly what is going on in the mind of the Negro. Does he not think? Does not his mind function in the natural order? Has not the race attained the state of self-consciousness? Is not there then such a thing as the Negro mind? Does not the mind of the race act under the varied stimuli of its peculiar environment? Surely the Negro is thinking and thinking seriously about his past, present, and future; thinking about the false political philosophy by which he has been condemned; thinking about the dominant Christianity by which he has on the basis of caste become acquainted with the white man's religion; and thinking finally about the democracy into the service of which he has been impressed but whose benefits he cannot enjoy; in short thinking that the white man is illiberal, unjust, and barbarous.

The white man is willing to concede that a few Negroes have such "silly thoughts" but contend that they do not voice the sentiments of the race. This, to be sure, is true to the extent that all Negroes do not take the situation equally seriously. But this disparity in thought obtains in all men who enunciated the principles by which change and reform have been effected in the development of nations. Many of these Negroes are now willing also not only to formulate principles but to direct the efforts of those who, peacefully if they can or forcibly if they must, will restrain the bloodthirsty from depriving them of their homes or their lives.

Some white men hearing these things say they do not care what the Negro thinks, for they are sure that the thought of the Negro will never be sufficiently potential to disturb the equipoise of the whites. But it would be well for a few of them at least to learn what a large representative majority of Negroes think of them. In the first place, few Negroes consider more than one white man out of a thousand anything but a hypocrite. It is difficult for a white man except by repetition of good deeds to convince the Negro that he is friendly to the race. The Negro is quick to regard what the white man does as an act of diplomacy which the Negro himself daily uses in currying favor with the white man to reach an end. The Negro has learned that the American white man is the most gullible being on earth and the fact that the Negro has been able to profit by this shortcoming of his white neighbor has enabled the unfortunate to extricate himself from many a serious difficulty.

In nothing do the Negroes as a whole doubt the white man more than as to his Christianity. Negroes attend the schools of the whites, undergo training for the ministry, secure from them funds for missionary work and for the construction of schools and churches, but because the whites have never lived up to the principles of the brotherhood of man, these same Negroes thus benefited seriously doubt the white man's profession to be a follower of the lowly Nazarene. White churches seem to Negroes not religious establishments but social centers prostituting the perverted teachings of Jesus to the promotion of caste within walls insured against attack by the special immunity granted because of supposedly common good resulting from the moral influences of the church in the community. A white minister is to the Negro no more an example of a man consecrated to God than is Vardaman or Blease an administrator of justice as revealed by God.[1]

Because of the incongruity between the white man's profession and practice there has been an increase in infidelity among Negroes. How can one expect the Negroes to maintain their faith in God when you insist that Lyman Abbott and Charles Parkhurst, who preach segregation, represent God?[2] What credence will the Negro give to the efficacy of the Christian religion, if you contend that in the United States one finds an example of a righteous nation, despite the fact that its policies are shaped by inconsiderate and narrow-minded prejudiced charlatans like William Howard Taft and Woodrow Wilson, who have no desire to rule justly but merely endeavor to serve efficiently the machines by which they are controlled.[3]

The Negro thoroughly understands the false political philosophy behind the whole system of government arrayed against the man of color. The Negro thinks of justice as absolute. The white sees it as a thing purely relative. Just as Christianity under the direction of the white man has become connected with the idea of blood kin, so has international law. It is in a sense the same idea that the Germans had in trying to subjugate the whole world, in attempting to enforce obedience to the will of the Teutons.[4] It is now dominant in the idea of the League of Nations as brought out by Woodrow Wilson, a compact to organize all of the powerful nations selfishly interested in their own welfare as was proved by the attitude of the Peace Conference in refusing to grant the request of Japan to eliminate race prejudice as a factor in apportioning the benefits to result from this League of Nations.[5]

"Democracy then," the Caucasian might as well say, "is a thing for the white man." "What then is the white man," says the Negro, "but a barbarian belonging to the Middle Age?" A man feeling that the law by which he is bound limits his conduct to his own people; who deems it a crime to steal from members of his own race but a virtue to steal from others outside of his own clan; who considers himself guilty of murder if he kills one of his own group but believes that he has done a heroic deed if he takes the life of one of another group.

The Negro, therefore, has little faith in the so-called Christian civilization. He is not inclined to ascribe to this religion in its corrupted form the credit which it has received as the supreme and absolute in bringing the world to its present advanced stage. The Negro, a Christian himself, does not doubt the power of the principles enunciated by Jesus of Nazareth. He contends that this religion has not yet been tried. The Negro agrees with that writer who says that whites nailed Christianity to the cross. There is much doubt that actual Christianity ever existed in Europe and even if it did, it suffered an untimely death in transit across the Atlantic.

The Negro ascribes the credit for the progress of mankind to commerce, political ambition, the rivalry of nations, inventions, and wars promoting the contact of people and the reconstruction of nations. To this they feel that Africa though prostrate at present contributed her share and that the people of color have on the whole had as much to do with making the world as progressive as it is, as any other group on earth. They believe, moreover, that the world cannot attain its golden age until it accepts as a basis for home, church, and state the principle of the brotherhood of man in the realization of which the blacks far excel the whites.

The often repeated assertion of whites that when the Negroes will have been adequately elevated they will come into their own and witness the abolition of all of these distinctions does not always carry the conviction as to sincerity. This may be the case of the devils who believe in God and tremble because they do. The Negro tends to regard this as a temporizing expedient to keep them from making urgent demands for what belongs to them. They easily justify their suspicions when they think of what little these self-made prophets do to bring about the fulfillment of their prophecy. If white men of this prophetic foresight were actually interested in the race, they would at least fearlessly advocate the enlargement of the fields of endeavor for Negroes that they may have every opportunity for improvement.

Improvement here, however, means not to make the Negro a white man but to make him a better man. The Negro has no desire to be everything the white man is or to do everything he does. No two races subjected to differing influences can be exactly alike and improvement in either does not mean that one should be made like unto the other. White friends of the Negro should stop worrying because Negroes do not feel, think, and do as the whites do. The Negro is not a white man with a black skin. If the blacks were suddenly transformed in spirit into white people, the racial conflict which would ensue would give rise to a state of anarchy which would not only drench the soil with blood but would result in the extermination of a large portion of mankind.

The Negro thinks then that the so-called Negro problem is the white man's problem. Both races have much to do to effect a readjustment but the white race, being in control, holds the key to the solution of the problem. The whites have too long been dominated by leaders whose only contribution has been to find fault with the Negro. Merely to blame a man for some personal fault which has resulted in his affliction with a troublesome malady is a poor method for affecting a cure. The Negro, therefore, resents the insult that he is a problem because he is not acceptable to certain barbarians whose only claim to distinction is that a few generations ago they had the honor of enslaving the blacks and can with impunity murder them without fear of punishment.

The fact is then that the Negro is in the midst of a civilization of which he is not and does not desire to become altogether a part, because this so-called civilization of the white man is peculiarly the white man's only so far as he has perverted it. Insofar as it is desirable it consists of the accumulations of centuries, an aggregate of fragments drawn from all lands and nations of all times, selecting that which the majority considers best and eliminating what had not proved to be for the benefit of the majority. To such a civilization the Negro himself has made a large contribution, for civilization, as the intelligent Negro sees it, is not restricted to fine houses and gaudy dress nor to a philosophy or literature which fails to find books in the running brooks, sermons in stones, and good in everything.

Civilization with the Negro then is good only so far as it does good. That civilization is best which confers the greatest good on the greatest number. The so-called white man's civilization primarily concerned with promoting the interest of Europeans and white Americans becomes, therefore, decidedly inferior to that of some of the natives of the jungles. Passing through Europe or America one finds abundant resources productive of riches, cities of splendor inhabited by people of luxury and ease, and governments controlling dominions almost encircling the globe, all made possible, however, by forcing to a lower level the man far down or by enslaving, plundering, or exploiting the weaker peoples of other lands. This is not in itself progress for mankind. It is merely the centralization of power in the hands of autocrats.

The Negro is wise enough not to worship power. The Negro, well read in the story of the Bible and not yet convinced by the new theology, has not come to the conclusion that kingdoms can become too powerful to be destroyed. The overthrow of slavery was a striking lesson to convince the Negroes of the inevitable forces at work to reduce the haughty and the proud.

The unexpected collapse of the Hohenzollerns and Junkers has given the Negro hope that the same social upheaval on this side of the Atlantic may unexpectedly advance our civilization toward the realization of actual democracy.[6]

The Negro, however, does not think of taking up arms except in self-defense. He is not the anarchist developed among the oppressed of Europe, not the insurrectionary enthusiast stirring the multitude in Latin America. Yet the Negro is not a coward. If he has to fight he is not afraid to play his part in the right cause and he usually acquits himself with honor. Negroes no longer rely solely on Providence for the solution of their problems but they feel that in the struggle between right and wrong there are at work forces with which they must connect for the righting of their wrongs. Believing then in the justice of his cause, the Negro is willing conservatively to fight the forces arrayed against him while at the same time he is working out his own salvation without fear and trembling. In fact, no race under such adverse circumstances has been able to keep so cool. One man recently characterized the situation by saying that the Negroes can brave almost any danger or hardship, for any black man who can live in the South can fearlessly attack the Hindenburg Line.[8]

One would wonder then how the Negroes with

this attitude toward the white man can be so loyal to this country. Here again the white man does not understand the distinction which every Negro makes between the country and the ilk running it. When a Negro buys a War Savings Stamp or Liberty Bond he does not do so because of the love he has for Josephus Daniels or Woodrow Wilson.[9] The Negro loves the country and is willing not only to give it financial support but even to die for it, so great is the attachment to the native soil. On the other hand, he actually hates the gangrene jealous and clannish, autocratic Republicans and Democrats who are the same impediment to the triumph of democracy here as the Junkers were to the liberation of the peoples of Germany.

Notes

1   For sketches of Vardaman, Smith, and Blease, see page
    100 above. For their biographies, see William F. Holmes,
    The White Chief: James Kimble Vardaman (Baton Rouge:
    Louisiana State University Press, 1970); Dewey W. Grantham,
    Hoke Smith and the Politics of the New South (Baton Rouge:
    Louisiana State University Press, 1967); and Bryant Simon,
    "The Appeal of Cole Blease of South Carolina: Race, Class,
    and Sex in the New South," *The Journal of Southern History*
    62 (February 1996), 57-86.

2   Lyman Abbott and Charles H. Parkhurst were prominent
    religious figures and social reformers during the Progressive
    era. Abbott was editor of the influential *Outlook* magazine, a
    journal which had been less than supportive of racial equal-
    ity. Best known for fighting political corruption in New York
    City, Parkhurst was also considered a liberal. He signed a call
    that led to the establishment of the National Association for
    the Advancement of Colored People. Yet Parkhurst's racial
    liberalism was not nearly as thoroughgoing and steadfast as
    his signature on the historic call suggests. He also believed
    that African Americans should protest their conditions less
    and prove themselves worthy of rights—a position held by
    those right of center. Never one to spare criticism toward
    half-hearted supporters, Woodson called Parkhurst out for
    his shortcomings as a supporter of African Americans. See
    Louis R. Harlan, "The Southern Education Board and the
    Race Issue in Public Education," *The Journal of Southern
    History* 23 (May 1957), 193.

3   Woodson's view that the Republican President Taft and the
    Democratic President Wilson were both controlled by "ma-
    chines" reflects Woodson's belief that neither party took seri-
    ously the interests of African Americans or any other citizens
    outside their political circles. While Woodson's views were
    more extreme than those of most black intellectuals, others
    shared the growing view that African Americans were not
    being well served by either party.

4   Teutons were considered to be a Germanic race, especially by those Germans calling for German racial superiority.

5   While many other Americans faulted Wilson's promotion of the League of Nations for its liberality, Woodson noted its shortcomings from the perspective of non-white nations and peoples, critiquing its failure to respect and promote self-determination.

6   Woodson here refers to the Hohenzollern family of Germany, whose power had grown so great over the centuries that it led to the Kingdom of Prussia and the establishment of modern Germany in the nineteenth century, only to be dethroned as a result of Germany's defeat in World War I. The Junkers constituted the powerful landowning class in Prussia that dominated the politics of Germany, and, according to many, led to the country's defeat in World War I.

7   Here Woodson refers to the numerous movements against colonial and despotic rule in the region during the nineteenth and early twentieth centuries.

8   A term coined during World War I, the Hindenburg Line was an elaborate defensive fortification created by the Germans when they were being overwhelmed by the Allied forces.

9   Josephus Daniels was a Southerner appointed by President Woodrow Wilson as the Secretary of the Navy. He served during World War I.

10

What the Negro Wants

On an occasion during the French Revolution there was evoked the colloquy: What is the third estate? Nothing. What does it want to be? Everything. Nothing can more aptly summarize the demands of the American Negro today. He wants every right and privilege given any other citizen, every opportunity for moral, intellectual, and economic development, in fact, all that any man can hope for or attain. The Negro does not proclaim such demands from the house tops and certain prominent members of the race even pretend that Negroes are not struggling for social equality, but in the heart of every Negro is a longing desire impelling him to strive to reach this end. And what else can a sane man expect of a self-respecting Negro but that he should aspire to becoming economically free from the domination of trade unionism, socially free from insult, and politically free from peonage?

The Negro wants security against mob violence, immunity from the attacks of bloodthirsty barbarians who take human life for the sport of it. He cannot feel free to follow his daily course when he thinks of the three thousand Negroes who since the Civil War have met death at the hands of the whites and of the scores of Negroes now being annually dispatched to eternity in the same way. No Negro in the criminal communities knows when his wife or daughter will be insulted, when he for no apparent cause will be ordered to leave his home, or when it will be attacked and burned. The Negro demands then the abolition of the personality of law, the law of the barbarian raising the hue and cry to exterminate the unfortunate within the gates because he is not of the barbarian's kith or kin.

The Negro asks too for justice in the courts. If the substitution of court procedure for mob violence means after all that the accused brought before the tribunal is to be tried according to his color, the administration of justice does not thereby make a long step forward. Law as determined by the courts of some states becomes one thing for the white and a different thing for the Negro. In many sections a Negro having an altercation with a white man usually gets a merciless beating from the white man's friends, if he happens to be fortunate enough to escape with his life, and if brought into court, the Negro is usually punished to the full extent of the law whether he be guilty or not. The courts too, in collusion with the public and sheriffs, count on rounding up a definite number of Negroes for a fixed period to secure the treasury adequate fines and fees to make their positions worthwhile. So prevalent has this custom become and so disastrous have been the economic effects of this cruel treatment of the blacks that recently whites of the more hopeful class have themselves asked that an end be put to these nefarious practices.

The Negro demands likewise economic opportunity. The higher pursuits of labor so long closed to the Negro by pursuing mediaeval methods should be opened. He wants the chance to work and to invest his earnings profitably. Throughout the Negro is excluded from almost every pursuit which the white man by the aid of trade unions can monopolize. In the South the Negro has a better economic chance for the reason that the white man in that section is not inclined to labor except when absolutely necessary. It is unfair then to blame the Negroes for not living up to the same standards as those obtaining among other groups and at the same time limit his earning power by the demands of organized labor. No man should be expected to run with his feet tied. Rather than condemn the Negroes for what they do not do under these circumstances they should be commended for doing anything worthwhile in spite of opposition.

Another desire of the Negro is the removal of economic handicaps which have increased in the proportion that Negroes have learned to struggle upward. The rapid accumulation of wealth among Negroes has so startled the white man who has had all of his years of opportunity that he feels the necessity for placing obstacles in the way of those acquiring property lest they overtake the whites more favorably circumstanced. This is a rather strange comment on the much talked of superiority of the white race that this group should concede that the only way possible to prevent Negroes from surpassing them in an economic contest is to make it illegal for them to do so. This same spirit has actuated legislators to promote segregation by prohibiting Negroes from purchasing property in certain parts of districts, counties, or urban communities. Laws providing for such distinction have been declared unconstitutional by the Supreme Court of the United States but a public opinion among the whites to the contrary constitutes an unwritten law which only a material advance in civilization can remove.

The Negro asks also for the opportunity to educate himself. As a citizen and a consumer in the community he pays in the economic sense as much in taxes as any other citizen. Why then should the government spend one dollar for the education of the white child for every twenty-five cents it appropriates to the education of one of color? A Negro in the South sometimes cannot secure for the education of his children even the school tax derived from the assessment made on his own property. A part of this often goes to educate the white children of the community in schools from which his children are excluded. The Negro needs, moreover, not a mere makeshift provision for separate schools poorly equipped and conducted by incompetent teachers owing their positions to their ability to play the role of racial toadies. The Negro must have modern school structures and thoroughly educated teachers qualified to use education as the great leverage by which the belated class shall be elevated.

The Negro ardently desires the abolition of all laws providing for distinctions as to intermarriage. The objective of the Negro in this case, however, is not to facilitate the interbreeding of the races but to remove any restriction which differentiates between him and any other citizen. In the South where such laws exist they amount to no more than a rigid provision making sexual intercourse between white women and men of color impossible while women of color are left at the mercy of the white man. As no Southern state would enact a law compelling a white man to marry a woman of color whose honor he may sully, he has ample outlet for his vice through legalized concubinage. White men making this base use of women of color do not thereby lose their status as men of high standing in the community. Many men of this type have served high in the council of the state and nation even as members of Congress and presidents of the United States. The abrogation of these measures would liberate the woman of color from the fetters of moral lepers and would elevate the womanhood of the race.

The Negro wants above all the abrogation of Jim Crowism in schools, public places of recreation, on the street cars, and on the railroads. Separate facilities always mean that the Negro must have less than his white neighbor. Places of amusement are in their very nature agents of the body politic enjoying the protection and support of the government for the good they do the public. Negroes taxed to maintain the government should have access to them. The silly discrimination made in the separation of the races in the South on the street and railroad cars is a handicap to traffic, an unnecessary inconvenience to business and an unmerited humiliation of the helpless. When traveling, a busy man has no time to be seeking some special place to sit or stand and the community which takes up its time with such trifles may preserve this peculiar stamp of backward culture but must in the end fall behind in the onward march toward efficiency and achievement.

The Negroes are all but peremptory in their request for better treatment in the cafés and railway stations and in the sleeping cars. Negroes are in business just as other men and in having to do much going to and fro they suffer physically when denied the accommodations offered others en route. Traveling a long distance the Negro must sit up for days in going through those backward commonwealths where unwritten law prevents a man of color from sleeping in a Pullman car. When he is hungry he must wait until all the whites on the train have eaten or is told that he must not enter the dining car at all. Arriving at the station in a strange city the situation is the same. He cannot appease his hunger in the café in the station and no hotel except one of some Negro will receive him. As few Negroes are in a position to purchase the property required for such establishments near the station in large cities, the Negro tourist goes along the best he can inquiring his way until he finally finds lodging somewhere in the distant Negro quarter sufficiently far removed from the whites to insure them against contamination.

The Negro asks, moreover, for an open door to civil and political honors. He is according to the Constitution of the United States a citizen of this country and no state has any grounds for abridging his privileges and immunities on account of his color. As a matter of fact, however, the Negro is actually disfranchised throughout the South in that he is not allowed to vote at all or when permitted to do so his vote is not counted. This requires no argument to be condemned as a shameful procedure when the Negroes are not only taxed to maintain the government but are called upon to give their lives to defend this country.

Never were there exhibited nobler examples of heroism than by the Negroes during the World War. They contributed to the support of the War Relief Organization, freely bought War Savings Stamps and Liberty Bonds, and sent their sons to die in France for a democracy which they have hitherto known only as observers. Such heroes should have, must have the ballot. Any action to the contrary must brand this country as deficient in the moral fibre essential to greatness and doomed to the premature decay consequent upon the promotion of invidious social and political distinctions.

The Negro not only wants to be a voter to determine by his ballot who should administer the affairs of government which he must support, but he wants also to hold office himself. It is the public right of every citizen to hold office and the Negro must not be made an exception. The Negro race as a whole has never and will never advocate the exaltation of the incompetent to positions of honor. In the days of the Reconstruction they eagerly sought for office aristocratic white men and when they refused the Negroes sometimes had to make the best use of carpetbaggers or inexperienced Negroes. When in examination of candidates today, therefore, it appears as it may do that the Negro is the best qualified, his color should not bar him from the honor of serving his constituents in an official capacity. The record of men of color now in office and the extensive knowledge and experience of others learned in government and political science remove all doubt as to the Negroes' qualification and the country must rapidly get away from the position regarding the duty of statecraft as restricted to a governing class established upon the oppression of other orders of society, which must never hope to disturb the serenity of the favored few. Any other tendency will indicate a step backward, a movement away from the democracy of which we have recently heard so much and which we are now expecting to enjoy.

Equal opportunity in the army of this country is another demand of the Negro. If he has to fight, let him fight his way to the top. Since he must serve in the ranks in a segregated group let him serve under his own men. Against this there is a natural antagonism in this country. The South which is increasing persecution of the Negroes has done almost everything imaginable but to exterminate them and even that to some extent, in certain parts, has a horror for seeing the Negro under arms. What would the Negro soldiers do if they would turn on their oppressors—this has been a serious question to that section. The people of this country as a whole too have not been very enthusiastic about giving the Negro such encouragement. In times of great danger, however, the Negro has always been called on as was the case in the American Revolution, the War of 1812, the Civil War, and recently in the World War.

Such a policy, however, is decidedly unfair to a taxpaying people and none but an uncivilized group will adhere to it. If the Negro is to fight for this country why not train him at West Point and at Annapolis along with the whites? Such foresight will redound to the interest of the country in that it will result in the preparation of better soldiers to defend the nation. It is criminal to deprive the Negro of the advantages of military training and, when the country has reached its extremity, rush him into the mouth of the hostile cannon without adequate preparation. If the United States hopes to construct a military machine efficient enough to compete with those of Europe, caste in the army must go.

Much has been said about the Negroes' being good soldiers when they are well led. This intimation of the prejudiced white is that the Negro as a soldier, very much as the Negro as a slave, must have the white man for a boss. How difficult it is for a white man to realize the fact that he is no longer a slaveholder. Negroes accomplish most on their own initiative as they have since emancipation. The Negro soldier, therefore, finds delight in serving under an officer of his own color.

To contradict this truth, however, an officers' clique, supported by higher officials naturally prejudiced against the Negro, came to a secret understanding to discredit the Negro officer even before the Negroes went to France. In their official reports and correspondences, therefore, the Negro officers have, from the time they first received their commissions, been branded as arrant cowards disqualified because of the "lack of moral fibre and character inherent in the Negro race." Such a characterization has been applied to Negro officers who won distinction in battle in France as in the case of Lieutenant Thomas M. Dent, Jr. and Captain James Wormley Jones known among the French as heroes.[1] In conformity with the wishes of the prejudiced autocrats in the army, however, the War Department has proceeded to demobilize Negro soldiers and officers who desire to remain in the army as the pro-rata belonging to one tenth of the population. Is this the democracy for which France bled? Is this the share of it that the Negro must receive for the millions they subscribed to support the government and for the lives which they gave to defend the nation's honor?

The Negro finally asks that he be treated as a man. The white man must cease to regard him as an object of derision and insult. As long as the Negroes as a group are treated in any way as the inferiors of the whites there will always be the indiscreet and the unprincipled class on hand to impose disabilities and burdens on the despised to handicap them in their struggle upward. As one thoughtful Negro discussing the matter once said every time a white man teaches his child that it is dishonorable to address a Negro as mister he encourages him to join the mob to lynch him or to burn him alive. It is simply an illustration of sowing and reaping. Any effort to make it appear that it matters not how low a white man may be, he is after all superior to all Negroes, is the perpetuation of the race conflict, mob violence, and backwardness of the community thus afflicted by this unscientific and mischievous education. Let every Negro be considered not according to his color but according to what he has done or is doing for the good of his family, his community, and his country.

Notes

1 Woodson is undoubtedly referring to Lieutenant Thomas M.
Dent and Captain James Wormley Jones of Washington, D.C.
Jones would shortly thereafter return to the United States
government's employment as Agent 800 for Edgar Hoover,
infiltrating the United Negro Improvement Association and
reporting on the African Blood Brotherhood. See, Theodore
Kornweibel Jr., *"Seeing Red": Federal Campaign against
Black Militancy, 1919-1925* (Bloomington: Indiana UP,
1998), 132 and Winston A. Grady-Willis, "The Black Panther
Party: State Repression and Political Prisoners," in *The Black
Panther Party Reconsidered,* edited by Charles E. Jones,
(Baltimore: Black Classics Press, 2005), 364. Monroe Mason
and Arthur Furr, *The American Negro Soldier with the Red
Hand of France* (Boston: Cornhill, 1920).

About the Author

Carter G. Woodson was born on December 19, 1875, in New Canton, Virginia, a small town in Buckingham County. His parents, James Henry and Anne Eliza Woodson, were ex-slaves who owned a small farm. As a child, Carter G. Woodson, along with his siblings, worked to support the family and was able to attend school only irregularly. In his late teens, he moved to West Virginia, where he labored building railroads and then in a coal mine. Just before his twentieth birthday, Woodson started high school.His quest for knowledge led him to Berea College, Lincoln University, the University of Chicago, the University of Paris, and Harvard University, where he completed his doctorate in history in 1912.

For a decade, Woodson taught in the public schools of Washington, D.C. He served as dean at Howard University and West Virginia Institute before retiring from teaching in administration.

Woodson spent the bulk of his career building the Association for the Study of Negro Life and History, which he established in 1915. Founded on the idea that people of African descent had to correct the historical record and demonstrate their role in history to take their proper place in the world, the Association established the *Journal of Negro,* now *The Journal of African American History.* In 1926, Woodson initiated Negro History Week, which an increasing portion of the world now celebrates as Black History Month. In 1937, at the urging of Mary McLeod Bethune, he established *The Negro History Bulletin,* now *The Black History Bulletin,* for teachers and younger readers. Woodson's desire to put the truth about peoples of African descent before the world led him to incorporate The Associated Publishers in 1921.

Woodson authored and edited numerous books. They include *The Education of the Negro Prior to 1861* (1915); *A Century of Negro Migration* (1918); *The Negro Church* (1921); *The Negro in Our History* (1922); *The Negro as Businessman* (with John H. Harmon, Jr. and Arnett G. Lindsay, 1929); *The Negro Wage Earner* (with Lorenzo Greene, 1930); *The Rural Negro* (1930); *The Mis-Education of the Negro* (1933); *The Negro Professional Man and the Community* (1934); *The African Background Outlined* (1936) and several others.

Woodson's work and intellectual interests carried him from the Philippines to Africa. In common with many of his generation, Woodson was a Francophile, delighting in French plays and literature. He won numerous awards, including the NAACP's coveted Spingarn Medal in 1926. Woodson remained a bachelor, and kept close ties with his relatives throughout his life. He passed away on April 3, 1950.

About the Editor

Daryl Michael Scott is Professor of History at Howard University. He received his bachelor's degree from Marquette University and a doctorate from Stanford University in 1994. His *Contempt and Pity: Social Science and the Image of the Damaged Black Psyche* (Chapel Hill, 1997) won the Organization of American Historians' 1998 James Rawley Prize for the best book on race relations.

Since joining the Executive Council of ASALH in 2003, he has reorganized the *Black History Bulletin* as a journal for teachers by teachers, founded and edited *The Woodson Review,* established the ASALH Press, redesigned and served as webmaster of the ASALH website, instituted and maintained ASALH's online store and convention websites, and re-edited Woodson's *The Mis-Education of the Negro.* He is currently president of ASALH.

Index